GOD

HEINRICH OTT

Translated by Iain and Ute Nicol

JOHN KNOX PRESS
ATLANTA

Published simultaneously in Great Britain by The Saint Andrew Press,
Edinburgh, Scotland, and in the United States by John Knox Press,
Richmond, Virginia.

This book was originally published in German, *Gott* © Kreuz-Verlag,
Stuttgart, 1971.

Library of Congress Cataloging in Publication Data

Ott, Heinrich.
  God.

  Bibliography: p.
  1. God.
BT102.O8613   211   73-5350
ISBN 0-8042-0590-6

Second printing, 1975
Printed in the United States of America

Contents

Theism and post-Theism

It is becoming quite evident that the question now at the centre of Christian and of theological thinking is the question of God. The question of God—this involves a whole complex of very elementary questions such as: *Does God exist? What does God mean for our lives? What does it mean to speak of God?* These questions, more than any others, are the questions which theologians, students of theology and Christians have to face. At the present time, something like a worldwide theological culture is beginning to take shape. It runs through the different confessions, countries and continents. Everywhere the same big problems are being discussed. For example, the response to John A. T. Robinson's book *Honest to God* (1963) was world-wide. The discussion of the provocative theological thesis which proclaimed the 'Death of God' was also worldwide. The debate continues today, although in my view this is no longer to the same extent the focal point of general interest which it was only a few years ago. Nevertheless, the question which gave rise to this debate has been all the more powerfully impressed upon our consciousness, and that question is the question of God.

In our modern mass society and in our technological world people not only have doubts about a *gracious* God (like the young Luther); they simply no longer have any certainty about God at all. They feel that they are faced with the possibility that the whole of reality is meaningless. They find themselves confronted with a world which runs like a machine and which, in the end, aimlessly and without purpose or meaning, will wear itself out like a machine. Our task therefore, the task of Christian thinking in this age, is to pose the question of God anew, the God of the Fathers who reaches out to us and who does not let us go, the God of Bonhoeffer and Pascal, of Luther and Thomas Aquinas, and of Augustine and the Bible (to name only a few of the faithful witnesses whose voices may still be heard). At the same time the task is to discover this God anew, or, as the Psalmist puts it, 'to seek God's face'. For in my opinion everything depends upon our continuing to understand this God as personal. For it is not just 'God' (the word is open to many different interpretations), but 'God as Person' which stands at the centre of discussion and which has become questionable. For modern man, the difficulty is not so much that he is unable to grasp that behind everything he can positively know he may recognise an ultimate, ungrounded depth which demands his complete involvement. The real problem for our contemporaries is rather that they find it so difficult to agree with the words of Psalm 8:

> When I look at *Thy* heavens, the work of *Thy* fingers,
>   the moon and the stars which *Thou* hast established;
> what is man that *Thou* art mindful of him,
>   and the son of man that *Thou* dost care for him?

This is the challenge of Christian faith in God which has become so difficult to understand, namely, that the individual should have the reason and the courage to have personal dealings with a personal God.

But this is precisely what all the Fathers did. They walked with God in prayer and in the hearing of his Word. They knew that they stood before his face. They trusted in his promises and awaited the granting of their requests. What they called their faith found its consummation in no other way. And is it not the case that concepts so fundamental to Christianity and the Bible such as Word of God and prayer lose their basis and threaten to become meaningless apart from the notion of a strictly personal relationship between God and man? This point is basically very simple, in fact almost trivial. For not only the Word of God (the fact that God speaks), prayer (man's speaking to God), but also such notions as trust, obedience to God, the judgment, grace, mercy and righteousness of God and many other leading ideas of the Bible which are to be found in both the Old and New Testaments, belong semantically within the realm of the interpersonal. These are the sort of things that happen between persons, and it is from this context that such terms are derived. The problem, however, becomes difficult enough when we recognise that although God is certainly personal, he is nevertheless not the same as a human person. Therefore all those terms in which the Bible clearly speaks of God in his relationship to man have a symbolic character. In their reference to God and his action, they cannot have exactly the same meaning as within the sphere of the interpersonal. (For further discussion of this problem see Chapter 5.) But if we were to make a complete break with the realm of the inter-personal and wholly relinquish the presupposition that God is in some sense personal (my discussion throughout the whole of the present study should help to clarify in what sense), then it would be extremely difficult to see what such expressions could possibly signify at all, and we would have to ask whether or not the entire theme of the Bible would vanish along with them.

This understanding of God and this relationship to God which is so integral to the Bible and the Fathers is one which should not be prematurely abandoned in view of the very real doubt which is so characteristic of our time. A Christianity without God, which in my view some of our contemporaries have somewhat rashly propagated, runs the risk of falling well below the spiritual and existential standard of faith in God, the faith which polemicists nowadays fondly refer to as theistic. Even if we agree that 'isms' are relatively unimportant, never-theless, the content of Christian theism perhaps throws much more light upon our lives than any a-theism. And the questions we ask about standards and levels are by no means far apart from those which we ask with regard to *truth*. The fact is that it is at the deeper level with its greater power to cast light upon our existence that we also find ourselves closer to the truth. And the final truth about the varied nature of human life cannot be banal!

Some contemporary Christian theologians who have adopted an a-theistic or post-theistic position (or who believe that they must think in these terms) have, in my opinion, drawn up a quite naive and cheap picture of theism and of the faith of the Bible and of the whole Christian tradition in a personal God whose action is personal. They have sketched the picture of a being beyond the world, conceived wholly in human terms, of a 'Father beyond the starry heavens' who 'rules everything so wonderfully'. This is why such a primitive, anthropomorphic image of God could be so easily discarded. But what is it that one receives in exchange for this when one has decided not to be an atheist, but rather an a-theist who does not wish to turn his back on Christianity? The vague, barely conceivable and hardly articulable concept of an impersonal God who is described as 'the depth of being', 'the Whence of my being driven around' and such like. As far as I can see, no-one among these theologians has opted for a straightforward pantheism or deism evidently because such views must be considered to be too metaphysical.

Now the question is really whether it is worthwhile giving further consideration to a concept so lacking in content as this, and whether it would not in fact be wiser to remain silent about God altogether. This is not to adopt a plain atheism. It might be the silence implied in one's sense of the mysterious nature of that which transcends the forms of human thought and speech. (I am thinking here, for example, of *Ludwig Wittgenstein's* attitude to religious questions.) However, if one is silent about God, and if as a theme God is excluded entirely, the question would then be whether it would be possible at the same time to retain the proclamation of Jesus as a valid existential message for all men, or whether the better course (because clearer and intellectually more honest) would not be to recognise that the Jesus-tradition, however outstanding and effective in world history and in the history of ideas, represents only one phenomenon among others. Then, as an ideal, Socrates and his proclamation (for such a proclamation *de facto* exists), could well be regarded as of equal value with Jesus and his proclamation as the ideal. The standpoint and teaching of a modern follower of Socrates could prove to be an extremely wholesome and fruitful contribution to the social and political struggle of the present. Such a view could lend powerful theoretical and practical encouragement toward the humanisation of man. And considering the high standard of this particular position and the tremendous humanistic possibilities of the message of Socrates, I for one, were I a post-theist, would have serious misgivings about opting for Jesus rather than Socrates.

Moreover, as far as the Socratic history of traditions is concerned, our situation is surprisingly similar to our position with regard to Jesus. We possess no direct message from either of them, but only a posthumous, inspired, and to that extent not entirely authentic, witness. With Plato, Socrates is the 'Proclaimer who became the Proclaimed'. And it is this which Rudolf Bultmann has established about Jesus.

What I am concerned to defend with these considerations is certainly not what present day post-theists would wish to label 'the theistic presupposition'. That is to say, I am not asserting that one must *legitimize* the message of Jesus by presupposing a theistic picture of God. I am affirming quite the opposite: that properly understood in its real sense, the message of Jesus must be theistically *interpreted*, namely, as a Word *of God*, and, quite logically, as the Word of a God who can speak. Interpreted as the Word of God (and the proclamation of Jesus itself calls for this), the message of Jesus possesses an unsurpassable existential validity. On the other hand, if it is interpreted as a human utterance (because one no longer cares to reckon with a God who speaks), then, from the perspective of our contemporary historical situation (and we have no perspective other than this), the message of Socrates for example, may be judged to have an equal if not superior value when compared with that of Jesus.

In my opinion, the only really carefully worked-out model of a post-theistic theology is that presented by *Paul Tillich*. This project originated before the slogan 'death of God' had become part of the theological discussion. Its strength and clarity of conception lies in the way in which it develops precisely that view which present day post-theists were eager to avoid, namely, a distinctly metaphysical and ontological basis for all talk of God. God is 'being-itself'. He can be spoken of only symbolically, and the understanding of God as personal represents only *one* of those possible symbols.

However, I am bound to say now that I find Tillich as suspect as I do all post-theists. For it seems to me that because of the primitive picture of what they call theism, they have made it impossible to grasp the full existential depth of theism and its profound value for our thinking and for our lives, the theism which understands God as personal and which is to be found in the Bible and in the greater part of the Christian tradition. This is the reason why they have not given really serious thought to the theme which I shall formulate here in terms of the following problem and which I shall examine from different perspectives in the course of the following chapters:

Is it conceivable and meaningful, and, does it provide any new insight into reality, to suppose that every man and all men together stand over against a Person who possesses none of the attributes of finitude which we otherwise perceive in all other persons whom we encounter?

Is it not true that this idea has a power to illuminate our self-understanding and that without it this illumination cannot otherwise be found? This is not the place for blunt assertions. However, I would suggest (and this is a suggestion which must be confirmed step by step), that if we renounce the understanding of God as personal, then not only do certain quite definite possibilities and dimensions of human existence disappear, they can no longer be studied with the same lucid and binding power. What about forgiveness, for example; the setting free of the guilty? What would this be without a God who pronounces acquittal? Nevertheless, life in the freedom of forgiveness *is* a possibility for man—and it is also a reality in human life! And even if the reality of a personal God is accepted only as a postulate (and on the level of thought and theory, apart from its practical confirmation in the life of the individual, it can in fact never be more than a postulate), it is nevertheless a postulate with more power to illuminate our lives than any other interpretation of human existence, and it is of course part of the business of the theologian to show that this is the case. It enables us to understand better the enigma of man. It does more justice to what man is. And it is this which demonstrates the strength of the theistic postulate. Consequently, whether an individual wishes to live with this postulate, and then finds that he can live with it in such a way that for him personally it ceases to be merely a postulate, is clearly a question which lies outside the province of informative theological reflection.

Psychologically it is intelligible that a Christian should hold to the message of Jesus, and, on the other hand, be impressed by the spirit of many of his contemporaries whose doubt inclines them to the view that they can no longer believe in an invisible God. It is understandable that, in a situation such as this, a Christian may try to hold to the message of Jesus and at the same time discard the presupposition of a personal God understood in the traditional sense. It is also intelligible that this course can be taken even when he has not yet thought through the dimensions and the inner possibilities of a personal understanding of God. It is understandable that the person who attempts this, if he wishes to retain the message of Jesus, does not tend to express the negative side of his position in such clear and unambiguous terms as to assert: 'There is no God'. He rather prefers the milder, less clear and more ambiguous statement: 'God is dead'. However, no matter how understandable this enterprise may be, it must remain marked by this lack of clarity in thought quite simply because for Jesus himself, God (the *Father!*) was not a side-issue. The question about the further problem as to whether we must reckon with such things as a change in man's experience of God in different historical epochs, and, by inference, possibly with a transformation of God himself, will be examined below in a chapter devoted to this particular theme.

At the present time God is in question also within Christian theology itself. For this reason, the discussion about God today might easily become, and perhaps must become disputatious. The accomplishment of the post-theistic theologians is undeniable, for they have succeeded in bringing theological discussion back to its central and fundamental theme. In the following chapters I have neither wished nor been able to withdraw from the polemicising tendencies of this situation. Besides, one cannot simply 'provide information' about God. Nevertheless, those who care to be informed about the *discussion* about God are compelled to participate in it from the standpoint of a commitment. Therefore in what follows, I have taken up an unambiguous position in favour of the theism of the tradition. This is the position which I certainly regard to be the clearest and most fruitful for our thinking. The chapters which deal with what appear to be the merely traditional themes and questions such as the proofs for the existence of God or the doctrine of the Trinity are also to be seen in terms of their relation to this position which I have adopted. Personalism as a lived reality is already given with the biblical message, the life of Christian faith, and within the Christian community. The theological task to which I have devoted myself is to develop this within the context of the current discussion of the question of God and to define it as clearly as possible.

Chapter One

The Eclipse of God

(On the situation of faith in God in our time)

Today, the person who wishes to speak of God or reflect upon God must be clear about one thing: *in our time, God has become question-able.*[1] What does this mean? The sentence is ambiguous. On the one hand it implies that in our time, and to this extent it may possibly differ from others, the existence of God is not assumed to be self-evident. On the other hand, the fact that God is *question-able* can also mean that there is a special reason why our age should enquire after and seek God with particular urgency. Whoever takes it upon himself to speak of God, whether as a preacher or as a theologian, and absolutely refuses to take this fact into consideration, then for those of his contemporaries who are concerned about the question of God, his speech will remain unconvincing.

Basically, one may attempt to clarify the situation of our own day in two ways. There are sociological analyses as well as theological interpretations of all the things with which our own particular age confronts us. Around 1966, a 'Christian-atheistic' theology which was to become extremely popular made the declaration that God is dead, that he has died, in our history, in our culture, in our existence. This is in fact a theological interpretation which covers our entire cultural and spiritual situation. However, this does not enable us clearly to understand the situation nor does it adequately describe it. A parallel movement in European theology falls into the same style of summary theological interpretation when, for example, it arrives at the following statements: ... 'the "death of God" (is)

[1] Note: With the German 'frag-würdig' Ott wishes to suggest not only that God is in question, but also that the question of God is a question *worth* asking.

an event which has taken place within the last two centuries of European history and which conditions every aspect of life . . . (it is) a concrete event in history.' And further: 'an increasing number of people are so gripped by this experience that they can no longer reconcile it either with theism or atheism because these two positions alike betray a naive, undisturbed ideological confidence.' And again: 'The phrase "death of God" is meant to give theological expression to these changed psychosocial conditions. It points to the experience of the end of all immediate certainty, whether objective and universal or subjective and private.'[1]

On the other hand, one discovery of sociological research is that out of 100 citizens of the Federal Republic of Germany between the ages of 18 and 70, 97 are baptised, yet only 68 believe in God.[2] Another example is Günther Kehrer's empirical study *The Religious Awareness of the Industrial Worker,* Munich, 1967, where it is stated: 'Almost half of those questioned affirmed the existence of God or of a somewhat imprecisely defined higher being.'[3] It is clear then that such faith in God held as a matter of principle should become unspecific and vague when at the same time other elements of the Christian faith are generally disbelieved.

But what is in fact the case? In our industrial age, what is it that has happened to faith in God? In our own day God has become questionable. When we confine ourselves to a consideration of the relevant facts, what does this transformation consist in? To judge by the available evidence, it would be too much to assert that the faith in God of former generations of Christians is no longer possible or no longer genuine. And it would also be going much too far to maintain quite bluntly that all the evidence points to the fact that God himself has died. On the other hand, what can be affirmed, and what can also be

---

[1]Dorothee Sölle, *Christ the Representative,* London, 1967, pp. 10–12.

[2]In *Der Spiegel,* 18, December 1967, in a report entitled 'What do the Germans believe?'

[3]p. 77.

easily shown with the help of some statistics is this, namely, that faith in a personal God, in a God who reaches into history, and in a God who hears and answers man, is in the western world nowadays no longer the self-evident, all-embracing framework according to which the majority of society thinks, acts and organises its life. The existence of God is no longer the generally accepted premiss, just as it is no longer the premiss which outsiders most seriously doubt. The biblical notion of a 'history of salvation', understood as God's dealings with and over against man, is no longer the framework within which most people orientate their lives nor is it the basis upon which they communicate with one another. Faith in God, that is, in a higher being is in some form still maintained by a considerable number of people today in countries which were formerly Christian. Nevertheless, the fact that its form is vague and imprecise, that it is no longer concrete and that it no longer has the definitiveness of a generally accepted dogma, must necessarily mean *that God, that is, faith in God, ceases to be an active force in society and in history*. A Pope's power of excommunication would hardly cause alarm to any worldly ruler today. And although this was once the case, it no longer carries any serious political weight. The 'world of the beyond', the dwelling-place from which God rules is no longer an accepted reality. The individual no longer takes it into account, as he does this world, in working out a plan for his life. The idea of returning to the past and withdrawing into a monastery, or of dedicating oneself to works of piety in order to settle life's accounts, may once have been the accepted way. Today such notions are strange to us. In the same way, wars are no longer waged from motives of Christian piety. In the case of the present conflict in Northern Ireland, the real motives are to be sought not so much in the religious as in the social sphere.

Whatever the individual believes or disbelieves is no longer a matter of public interest. Faith has become a private matter and to this extent so also has God. He is outside the realm of relevant public discussion and for this reason has no repercussions on public life. For example, one doctor in a country town may privately be an atheist, another may go regularly to church, and a third may well be quite unsure about what sort of position he should adopt to everything. This may be so, yet the three may respect each other as colleagues. Perhaps the one may not even know what kind of attitude the other takes to these questions. Here there are no more class or educational norms. And the general situation described here is no different even when the church and when Christian motives make the headlines (as frequently happens in the case of the *Kirchentage*!). In the industrial society of the present it is doubtless true that many people are concerned about religious questions. To draw a picture of modern man becoming more disinterested in ultimate questions would be a simplification. However, this hardly alters the fact that faith in God, and the 'Christian world-view' which has its foundation therein no longer receive the same general public recognition which they once enjoyed in the Christian west. Where today would a confessing Christian, a Christian teacher or witness, employing arguments derived from the Bible, admonish a worldly ruler or a bearer of mandatory power in the name of God in the way in which Luther did, for example? Or like the *Antistes* of the old Zürich church since the time of Zwingli, with the accepted and permanent right to reprimand the town-council?

On the other hand, it is obvious that today there are also certain general premisses shared by everyone which few people would seriously question. They are recognised as the accepted points for the orientation of life and they act as the guidelines for everyone's design for life. It is in terms of such premisses that people communicate with each other simply as a matter of course. Everyone knows that there is general agreement about them. Such accepted premisses which are powerfully active in society and which have important consequences in the sphere of public life today, are, for example, faith in the reliability of scientific knowledge or trust in the power of technology. Even the person who himself does not know and cannot accomplish such things, knows without any doubt that 'it can be known, and it can be done'. Such power to shape the meaning and to determine the course of society once belonged to man's faith in God and to the fundamental view of a history of salvation.

When we look impartially at the present social phenomena of what was once the Christian west, these are the conclusions which emerge. On the other hand, on the basis of such discoveries, it would be rash to make definitive judgments about the nature of man's present or former 'religious experience', or about the forms and possibilities of his experience of God in former ages as compared with the forms and possibilities of such experience today. It would seem, however, that Dorothee Sölle is aiming at something like this when in the book to which we have already referred she writes: 'God has changed. What happened to Moses at the burning bush belongs to an irrevocable past. What St. Francis felt and experienced is no longer open to us to experience as something immediate. Luther's anxieties can be explained by the psychoanalysts and stripped of their unconditionality. The progressive awakening of the consciousness has excluded these possibilities of attaining certainty about God.'[1]

What is being affirmed here is that formerly, the experience of God was immediate, but that today, such immediacy is lost forever. But is it open to us to view the innermost nature of what the experience of God once was? Can we see into the innermost reality of a person's experience of God today? And is it possible for us to make any genuinely valid and final typological comparisons in this connection? (Of course we stand closer to present-day experience in the sense that we can speak about a person's religious experience with our contemporaries, we can hear that person's account of it and question him about it.) But can we already know what we, in our technological world, will be able to re-experience in the future? In any case, statements like these about religious experience have no real basis in the evidence before us; nor do they have any basis in the fact to which we have just referred, namely, that God and

[1] Op. cit., p. 140.

faith in him have become private matters, with the result that the power of faith to determine the shape of society has dwindled.

However, even though the facts which can be discovered about the whole problem of the question of God at the present time are external, and although they do not enable us to penetrate to the innermost reality of the experience of God, they are nevertheless of decisive importance. This is why the Christian preacher must involve himself with them, and this is why he has a duty to do them proper justice. He cannot in the end with a good conscience talk around them, nor does he have any right to ignore them. Whoever takes his place in the pulpit or at the rostrum and plans and formulates his sermon or theological lecture on the mere assumption that there is a God, that there are such things as God's history with man, such things as sin, a judgment and so on, and speaks simply because he thinks he can and must speak; whoever argues, rebukes, warns and comforts in such a fashion today will be unable to touch the lives of his hearers; he will fail to meet them in their honesty and sincerity insofar as they are honest and sincere. *The situation of God's question-ability calls just as much for a new style of preaching as it does for a new style of theology.* This style is one which consists not merely in blunt assertions and affirmations. It is rather the kind of style which points the way, the style of existential verification. Today, the person who speaks of God, whether in preaching or in doctrine and whether he is outside or within the Church, cannot retreat protesting: 'But it *is* generally assumed, or it is the accepted presupposition of some that there undoubtedly is a God'. Rather, in every thought and in every formulation connected with God, it must as far as possible be demonstrated anew *how* God is present and *in what way* he shows himself to be real, namely, through his entering into human life. This means that he comes to man with a specific claim, places him under obligation, points him in a particular direction and offers him a real chance. In other words: what must be shown is that if

God exists, *then this makes a real difference* for the person who believes in him. As long as the premises concerning the existence of God are no longer self-evident, then the theologian and the preacher today must always be prepared to strive anew and shoulder the difficulties which this 'showing' and this 'pointing' involve. The greatest weakness of Christian preaching and theology today is the naive way in which it is still assumed that these premises are foregone conclusions and the refusal to realise that they are no longer tenable. The theology of showing and of pointing, involving as it does this continual striving, is what in contemporary theology is known as the method of *existential interpretation*. And the concept in this sense was first employed by *Rudolph Bultmann*.

Nevertheless, when all these factors are taken into consideration, it immediately raises the question whether with the disappearance of these self-evident premises the Christian community has lost something, or whether in fact it may well have gained something . . .

However, for theologians at least, it is necessary to look for a theological interpretation of these factors. For the theologian, and every Christian as well to the extent that as a believer he is also a witness to his faith, must face the question: What is the meaning of this historical situation before God? What is his will for me, for us? What is it that in and through this situation he wants to say to us? We shall now look at three examples of theological interpretation, one Jewish, one Protestant and one Catholic:

1. *The Interpretation of Martin Buber*

What man experiences today is an 'eclipse of God'. This is the key-phrase (modelled on the constellation of an eclipse of the sun) which Martin Buber uses to describe the situation regarding the question of God and the experience of God in our time. With the help of his basic categories or relations, I-Thou and I-It, he interprets this situation in the spirit of our technological age. According to Buber's personalistic anthropology, man always stands in one or other of these basic relations to the reality which encompasses him; either in the relation of an I to an It or of an I to a Thou. In this connection Buber speaks on the one hand of 'primal distance', and on the other, of 'relation'. Both are basic to man's being. That man can view reality from a distance and make it into an object means that he is the creature who has a primal distance to the world. However, at the same time he also has the capacity continually to break through this distance and penetrate to the immediacy of the I-Thou relation. With the exception of one reality man always stands in the relation of I-It or I-Thou. That exception is God, who for Buber is the *absolute* Thou. He is the Thou who can never become an It. He is the eternal Thou in whom the lines of all I-Thou relations meet. And through every earthly I-Thou relation we are given a glimpse of the eternal Thou.

In this way Buber's anthropology and his theology are closely related. And it is against this philosophical background that he evaluates the situation of our own time as follows: 'In our age the I-It relation, gigantically swollen, has usurped, practically uncontested, the mastery and the rule. The I of this relation, an I that possesses all, makes all, succeeds with all, this I that is unable to say Thou, unable to meet a being essentially, is the lord of the hour. This selfhood that has become omnipotent, with all the It around it, can naturally acknowledge neither God nor any genuine absolute which manifests itself to men as of non-human origin. It steps in between and shuts off from us the light of heaven'.

These are the conditions which determine modern man's relationship to God. Nevertheless, as far as Buber is concerned, this situation is by no means final (which is quite the contrary to the view that 'God is dead'—for death is something final). It is really only the mark of our present epoch. As Buber says: 'Such is the nature of this hour. But what of the next? . . . The eclipse of the light of God is no extinction; even tomorrow that which has stepped in between may give way'.[1]

[1] *Eclipse of God*, pp. 166–167 (V. Gollancz Ltd., London, 1953).

2. *The Interpretation of Dietrich Bonhoeffer*

Dietrich Bonhoeffer dares to take a further step. In his view, the most prominent feature of our age, God's question-ability, is something which comes not from man, but from God himself:

> 'And we cannot be honest unless we recognize that we have to live in the world *etsi deus non daretur* (as though there were no God). And this is just what we do recognize —before God. God himself compels us to recognize it . . . God would have us know that we must live as men who manage our lives without him. The God who is with us is the God who forsakes us (Mark 15: 34). The God who lets us live in the world without the working hypothesis of God is the God before whom we stand continually. Before God and with God we live without God'.[1]

This famous passage from the prison letters is one to which the representatives of theological atheism frequently appeal. However, its profound dialectic is seldom fully appreciated. To distinguish the 'deus', who 'does not exist', from the 'true God', and to conclude that under the pressure of the times our concept of God must therefore be replaced by another, is to reduce what he really meant to an oversimplified piece of logic which can be all too easily resolved. It is suggested that we must exchange the now unacceptable theistic concept of God for a new, more genuine a-theistic understanding of God—for the God who is now called the 'depth of being' (John A. T. Robinson), or for the God who as such certainly 'does not exist' but who nevertheless, as it were 'encounters us in the event of our co-humanity'. This must therefore mean that although the theistic concept of God (the notion of a transcendent, personal God), may formerly have proved itself to be useful and meaningful, it has now become the meaningless and superfluous cipher for that which is and always was the essential thing, namely, for that which takes place between persons.

---

[1] *Letters and Papers from Prison,* Third revised and enlarged Edition, p. 196 (Letter of 16.7.44). SCM Press, London, 1967.

This somewhat superficial interpretation of Bonhoeffer's thought on this matter overlooks the apparent paradox which for Bonhoeffer himself is so important. For him, the 'God before whom we stand continually', and the 'deus' without whom we must live, are one and the same. Although Bonhoeffer was well aware of the a-religiosity of his time and even experienced it at a profoundly visionary level, he did not even consider the possibility of responding to this situation by exchanging the theistic (personal) concept of God for an a-personal concept of God. His entire life work, especially his later work, fully testifies to his own personal relationship to a personal God, to his prayer and his faith in the guidance and care of God: 'I believe that God is no timeless fate, but that he waits for and answers sincere prayers and responsible actions'. (From 'A Few Articles of Faith on The Sovereignty of God in History'.[1]) Many remarks to the same effect can be found, especially in the later Bonhoeffer.

However, Bonhoeffer had to face the fact that in our age, it is precisely this personal God who conceals himself. He himself constrains us to live 'before him' in such a way as to suggest that he does not *exist (etsi deus non daretur—Irrealis!)*. We are called upon to manage our own lives and the world, without recourse to God as a working hypothesis, that is to say, without the stopgap God who is always used to fill the gap when it is discovered that a certain problem cannot be solved. It is however rather the case that this God who conceals himself and who in a certain sense leaves us on our own, wishes to meet us not in the gaps or at the limits of our knowledge, but in the midst of our existence, and in our being with and for our fellow men.

Accordingly, God's withdrawal and concealment of himself in this a-religious age is for Bonhoeffer not merely something negative. It is at the same time something quite positive, namely, as a new disclosure, and as a new way of encounter with God. God gives us to understand that in our epoch, when

[1] Op. cit., p. 28.

man it seems can do everything, God discloses himself and is to be found not at the limits of human power (as for example when man finds himself at the mercy of nature), but in everyday human relationships. Incidentally, in *Martin Buber* we find again an interesting and impressive though seldom noted parallel to this situation which Bonhoeffer has in mind. In the essay 'Dialogue', Buber writes:

'Above and below are bound to one another. The word of him who wishes to speak with men without speaking with God is not fulfilled; but the word of him who wishes to speak with God without speaking with men goes astray.

There is a tale that a man inspired by God once went out from the creaturely realms into the vast space. There he wandered till he came to the gates of the mystery. He knocked. From within came the cry: "What do you want here?" He said: "I have proclaimed your praise in the ears of mortals, but they were deaf to me. So I come to you that you yourself may hear me and reply." "Turn back", came the cry from within. "Here is no ear for you. I have sunk my hearing in the deafness of mortals".

True address from God directs man into the place of lived speech, where the voices of the creatures grope past one another, and in their very missing of one another succeed in reaching the eternal partner.'[1]

The idea that the eternal God 'has sunk his hearing in the deafness of mortals' gives exact expression to that transformation which Bonhoeffer understands as the historical action of God in our contemporary situation. (For the concept of 'God's history' see Chapter 2 on the 'Transformations of God'.) It expresses the way in which God wishes to encounter us in the 'being with' and 'being for' of finite human beings.

[1] *Between Man and Man*, p. 33. Collins Fontana edition, London, 1961.

3. *The Interpretation of Karl Rahner*

The Catholic theologian Karl Rahner refers repeatedly to the 'experience of God's silence in our time'. (This, for example, is the theme of his essay, 'Why and How can we venerate the Saints', in *Theological Investigations*, Volume VII.) According to Rahner's understanding of God, God is not only the omnipresent, ineffable mystery encompassing and bearing man's existence. He is also the God who acts in history in his imparting himself to man and in that he gives man his life.

'Whether he openly expresses it or not, in his spiritual life man is always dependent upon a holy mystery as the ground of his existence. This mystery is the most primordial and the most apparent, yet for this very reason the most hidden and the most unheeded. The voice of this mystery is its silence, and in its absence it is there in that it points us to the boundaries of our lives. We call it God.'[1]

But the way in which this self-giving God approaches man in absolute love, and the way in which he permits himself to be experienced by faith are not the same in every historical epoch. As regards the present, Rahner writes: 'It is precisely for the really genuine believer that God has become incomprehensible and "distant" (even when the Christian himself knows that this incomprehensible and distant God is at the same time that freely self-giving mystery which is always near). Of course people have always known and recognised this fact. But our experience of this today is new and more radically acute. This is because the world has become immeasurably large and at the same time profane. In the everyday, unmiraculous experience of the world, God is not to be found as one datum among others. God is widely experienced as the silent mystery, infinitely ineffable and infinitely incomprehensible.'[2] Thus, according to Rahner, our own age has its own particular kind of experience of God. For Rahner this experience is epochal, in the sense that 'it is rooted in the situation of one's (i.e., modern

---

[1] *Schriften zur Theologie*, Band VIII, 1967, p. 159. (Not yet translated.)
[2] Op. cit., p. 287.

man's) own time.' This is to experience God as the silent mystery. This is emphatically not the experience of those who are indifferent to religion. It is rather, according to Rahner, the experience of the contemporary genuine believer. God himself deals with and encounters man *in our time* as the *silent One*.

It is worth noting that despite the different nuances, these comprehensive interpretations of our present situation, Jewish, Protestant and Catholic, worked out from the standpoint of faith, all point in the same direction. Common to all of them is that from the perspective of faith in a personal God, they seek to understand the situation concerning faith in God, a situation in which the personal reality of God has become question-able. In God's personal relationship to man something epochal has taken place which makes it appear that God is distant and absent. What then are the *theological consequences* of this fact which we have described and discussed in this first chapter, the fact that today in Christian thinking the problem of God's question-ability and the effect this has on faith are treated with such seriousness? The consequences, it seems to me, are threefold:

1. The question of God which is now at the centre of theology and of all Christian thinking raises the problem of whether there is a God, and, if God is, how we can speak of him meaningfully and intelligibly.

2. At the same time there is the idea of *co-humanity* (nowadays a concept which is quite frequently employed), the notion of man in his being together with others. It is recognised that it is with reference to this that the question of God and all our talk of God are to be measured.

3. At the same time it is becoming much clearer where *the real centre of the question of God lies*, and what it is that is really at stake in all the discussions between Christian theism and all forms of Christian or non-Christian a-theism. For in the end it is the more concrete question that really matters, namely, Is there a *personal* God, a God who speaks to and who answers man?

Some remarks of the Catholic theologian Henri de Lubac
provide a prospect of what is to follow and at the same time
are of some help in bringing our present discussion to a close:
'God is dead! Or at least so it seems to us . . . until we meet
him again around the next corner—alive. He makes himself
known to us anew, defying all that we have left behind us on
the way. These were just a few provisions for part of our
journey. They carried us part of the way until we came to the
point at which we had to make a new beginning . . . And once
we have really moved on, we shall find God himself even
greater. And yet it will be the same God. *Deus semper maior*. We
shall stride forward anew in his light—We never leave God
behind us . . . In whatever direction we go, he is already there
before us, calling us, and advancing to meet us . . .'

Chapter Two

Transformations of God

How then can it be that man's awareness of God and his relationship to God can change in this way? There is the change we have just discussed, the fact that we have reached an epoch in which man is experiencing an eclipse of God. A further change may take place in the epoch yet to come. It is possible that then we may share a new encounter with God, an immediacy of the experience of God which we have hardly yet imagined. We have spoken of the mark of our time as an 'event of God's history'. In the same way the three theological interpretations of our situation which we have examined also stress this point, namely, that the epochal character of this event is bound up essentially with God and even brought about by God himself.

What sort of perspective does this assume? What kind of notion of God and man permits us to think of such a transformation in our relationship to God? It would be easy enough to answer this question simply from the point of view of the history of ideas. We could say that in the course of time man's religious views and his views of God change, that they change within the bounds of particular religions such as the Christian religion itself. Thus, it might be said, man's relationship to his God is in fact always a series of different experiences. Now the question as to what God really is, or if he exists at all, can on this view be set aside. However, the theologian can hardly be satisfied with this way of approach. His concern is God *himself,* and he must ask whether and to what extent the transformations in man's awareness can have anything to do with God himself. Thus in contemporary theology one of the problems we face is the problem of the transformations of God.

In his book, *What kind of God?* Heinz Zahrnt writes: 'A theology *without* God is either pure anthropology or it is nonsense.'[1] And again: . . . 'anyone who thinks logically cannot avoid the honest alternative; either God is dead, in which case he has never lived; or else God has lived, in which case he is not dead. *For God cannot die!* "A god who can die deserves no tears", says Harvey Cox. We would go on to say: because he has never existed! The assertion that God is dead contradicts the inner logic of the idea of God, which is binding even on non-believers when they think of God.'[2] It is difficult to avoid the force of this simple logic. And it is salutary when occasionally a simple logic should be given its due place in the struggle against the menacing confusion of theological language. Nevertheless, the post-theistic theologian would not be so easily satisfied with Zahrnt's conclusion. He would argue the case that our age is under a historical constraint, and that as a human being he is bound to think of the God of the fathers as silent, absent, and even, dead. But the force of this compelling logic does not easily capitulate to the view that there is a certain historical pressure which controls the times in which we live. Still, we must pursue this matter further and ask why, in our historical epoch, it is necessary to talk about God in this way.

The post-theistic theologian, Gert Otto (in his book *Reason, Aspects of Modern Faith,* Vol. 5, in the series 'Theological Themes'),[3] has, with the help of the notion of the transformations of God, attempted to reinforce his thesis that 'a reasoned faith poses questions which reach beyond the personal and metaphysical understanding of God'. He writes:

'Does this mean that the distance between ourselves and the biblical understanding of God has become too great? Can we still claim to be able to speak of God in a biblical way? It is precisely this which must be advanced against those who can only reiterate the language of the Bible. And that to which

[1] *What kind of God?* p. 41. (SCM Press, London, 1971).
[2] Op. cit., p. 40.
[3] Not translated. Ger. title: *Vernunft.*

Rudolph Bultmann was referring when some years ago he adopted Barlach's talk of the transformations of God has been described in minute detail by Werner H. Schmidt with regard to the Old Testament understanding of God:

"In the course of time this faith did not remain the same; for it is bound up with the situation in which it stands. It does not merely make its appeal to history. It is itself history and is grasped by its movement . . . In the strict sense there is nothing constant in history, nothing which is not open to change".

Our present task is to do justice to this dynamic understanding of history (which, it must be noted, we cannot conceive of apart from the Old Testament heritage), in its relationship to the problem of God. For in the most fundamental sense, God and man's history do not remain separate from one another. They are in fact so interwoven that they condition one another.' [1]

These brief remarks amount to little more than mere assertions. We must go further than this, and as far as the (ontological) background of such a view is concerned we must ask: *How is it really possible to conceive of such a thing as a transformation of God? At what sort of level does this take place?* For one thing it is clear that this whole way of thinking is based upon one strong objection to the theological tradition, namely, the idea of God's absolute immutability. God is perfect; in him there are no unrealized possibilities and therefore no becoming. That God, the eternal One, should be subject to change, is just as inconceivable as that he should be subject to death.—Or by comparison with this view, should God be thought of as a being in process of development, as coming wholly to himself and to perfection only gradually and by means of a process to which we also contribute with our lives, our decisions and our sufferings? This idea of a 'God who becomes' has certainly made its appearance in certain forms of mystical or philosophical religiosity, but as far as I can see, it has no basis whatever in the biblical witness to God. In the Bible, in the

[1] Op. cit., Ger. pp. 79f.

Old Testament as well as in the New Testament, it is certainly true that God is eminently 'historical', that is to say, he is constantly bound up with man in his history. Nevertheless, this is not to say that he needs man in order to become wholly perfect. He becomes man's partner in history, but man is not necessary to his perfection.

If we reject this possibility, how then can any talk of the transformations of God be meaningful? I shall cite here the most important statements of three theologians who have given expression to their views on this question. Again we shall see that there is a remarkable agreement among them.

Rudolph Bultmann writes: 'We must seek and find the unconditional in the conditional, the beyond in this world, the transcendent in things present. And we must always remain open for encounters with God in the world and in time . . . and in the changing situations of our lives.' [1] (See also the passage from G. Otto quoted above.) This is the real meaning of the mythological notion of a transformation of God. God, that is, changes in that he enters human history, encounters man *in* history in historical, human form. For Bultmann therefore, the classic New Testament passage with regard to the notion of the transformations of God is Matthew 25: 31–46, the parable of the great judgment, and especially the saying: . . . 'as you did it not to one of the least of these, you did it not to me.'

In a meditation on the theme 'God became man', Karl Rahner deals with the following question: Can God really *become* anything? Rahner reaches the conclusion that, 'If we face squarely the fact of the incarnation, which our faith testifies to be the fundamental dogma of Christianity, we must simply say: God can become something; he who is unchangeable in himself can *himself* become subject to change *in something else*.' [2] 'Subject to change in something else' means that God, insofar as he is the partner of another, namely, man's partner in history and man's covenant partner, can change,

[1] *Glauben und Verstehen*, Vol. IV, pp. 125f.
[2] *Theological Investigations*, Vol. IV, p. 113.

become something, *in* this historical relationship. God does not stand aloof from this historical relationship. In the end it is not a matter of indifference to him. He himself has entered this history as a genuine partner.

Finally, perhaps it is Martin Buber who expresses the matter in the most suggestive way when he writes: 'You know always in your heart that you need God more than everything; but do you not know that God needs you—in the fullness of his eternity needs you? You need God, in order to be—and God needs you, for the meaning of your life. In instruction and in poems men are at pains to say more, and they say too much— What turgid and presumptious talk that is about "the God who becomes"; but we know unshakably in our hearts that there is a becoming of the God that is. The world is not divine sport, it is divine destiny.' [1]

These three thinkers are all saying basically the same thing: God stands in a historical relationship with man. Apart from this relationship we could not conceive of him at all; nor would he be real for us. And it is because this is an actual and not an apparent history, a history *between* partners and which is of concern to both partners, that God transforms himself in it. This does not mean that we should entertain the objective notion of a God who becomes and who grows (in the same way, for example, as a vegetable organism becomes and grows). It must mean, however, that important epochal changes do in fact take place in man's awareness of God (and it is always through man's awareness of God that God is mediated). These do not occur only on the human side. They are also to be understood as transformations of God in history, in the history of human encounter with him.

If God were really dead, he would have no more history. There would then only be man's history with himself. Therefore, any theologian who wishes to insist on the notion of the death of God can no longer appeal to this basically meaningful idea of the transformations of God. The notion of the trans-

[1] *I and Thou*, Second Ed. 1958, p. 82.

formations of God (to distinguish it from the pantheistic idea of a 'deity who becomes'), presupposes the historicity of God and man, and that they exist as partners in a living and intimate historical relationship. The term 'history' is meaningful only when this personal partnership is presupposed. We have no experience of a history between impersonal beings. To this extent the idea of the transformations of God is witness to the fact that God is personal. Again in this connection *Martin Buber* makes some interesting remarks in a reply to the American philosopher *Charles Hartshorne:* 'I have stated that God enters into a relationship with man. Because of this it has been said that God is therefore no longer absolute, but relative. The reason for this, Hartshorne argues, is that "the relative is defined by its dependent relationship to something else". But does an absolute being have to be unrelated to other beings?' Clearly, what Buber is saying here is that a relationship, a personal partnership between an absolute and a relative, between an infinite and a finite being can, and in fact does, exist.

Chapter Three

Proofs of God and Faith in God

How can we *know* God? How can we be certain of the God of the biblical and of the Christian tradition, a personal God (and at the same time supra-personal), who as such is able to enter into a historical relationship with man? This God who is 'capable of history' has always been the God of the biblical and of the Christian tradition, even though through the ages the images and concepts of God have undergone diverse changes. (I omit mention here of the mystical, unhistorical strand which is also to be found in the Christian tradition but which amounts to no more than a relatively small part of it.) In the theologies of former periods this question was answered in the following way: *that* God exists is something which can be proved conclusively by the natural means of reason which is at all men's disposal. This was the age which produced the notion of a *natural theology*, that is, of a knowledge of God on a natural basis and requiring no appeal to a supernatural revelation of God in his Word and in the Bible. On this view, apart from revelation and apart from faith, all men can at least know this much about God; they can know *that* he is, that he is omnipotent, omniscient, omnipresent and eternal, the ground and origin of the whole world. To know more of God than this is possible only to those who put their trust in divine revelation. But all men at least have access to this through experience and reason alone.

This was the way in which *Thomas Aquinas*, in his famous 'Five Ways' (*quinque viae*) sought to furnish proof of the reality of God. This has remained one of the decisive and controlling factors in Catholic theology to the present time. On this view it can be discovered and proved by the natural power of reason that God is:

1. The Prime Mover of the universe, apart from whom nothing else could possibly move;

2. The First Cause, apart from whom no other cause in the world could be effective;

3. The Necessary Being, that is, the being who cannot be said *not* to be, and apart from whom no other being (which can always in principle be said *not* to be) would be real;

4. The '*Summum bonum*', apart from whose existence it would be meaningless to speak of 'good' or 'less good'; and

5. The intelligent One who directs all things, and apart from whom the meaningful structure and process of the universe would be inconceivable.[1]

Almost two centuries before Thomas Aquinas, *Anselm of Canterbury* had also attempted a proof of the existence of God on a different basis. In his 'Five Ways' Thomas's starting-point is *experience*, that which we experience in the world, in the realm of God's creation. His five proofs of God are addressed to man's general, this-worldly experience: 'When you reflect upon your own experience you are yourself bound to admit that something must necessarily exist of which it cannot be said—as is the case with all other things in the world—that it could not exist. That which necessarily exists, we call "God"'—Or, you must grant that there must be a first cause. It is this first cause that we call "God", and so on'—By contrast to this Anselm of Canterbury chose a quite different starting-point for his famous proof of God's existence in the *Proslogion* (i.e., 'Address', so called because it is written in prayer-form in the second person). His starting-point is not our innerworldly experience, but rather the *concept* of God itself: whoever has the right concept of God, that is to say, whoever has grasped who or what 'God' really means, must also come to the conclusion that this God in fact actually exists. The right and appropriate concept of 'God' means: 'Something so great that nothing greater can be thought' (or, 'That than which nothing greater

[1] *Summa Theologiae*, Part I, Question 2, Art. 3.

can be thought'). If then this being than which none greater can be thought did not exist, it would not be that than which a greater cannot be thought, for then something greater could be conceived of, something which also in fact exists. *This* would therefore be that than which nothing greater can be thought. Consequently, God, as that than which nothing greater can be thought, must also *exist*.

To this argument for the existence of God *Immanuel Kant* objected that a hundred real dollars are no more than a hundred possible dollars. Thus it is mistaken to argue from the possible or conceivable existence of a highest being to the actual existence of this being. Kant also regarded Thomas's proofs of the existence of God as invalid. For although they take their starting-point in human experience, they reach speculatively beyond all human experience and arrive at assertions which so transcend every human experience that they can no longer be confirmed by the generally accessible and objective kind of experience which we have in the world. According to Kant, man's theoretical reason is competent only within the realm of innerworldly experience. Only in this sphere can it come to any firm conclusions. For Kant therefore, God's existence cannot be proved theoretically. It follows rather as a demand (as a 'postulate') of the moral life and from the facts of responsibility and conscience (a 'postulate of practical reason').

In his *Fides Quaerens Intellectum—Anselm's Proof of the Existence of God* (1931)—Karl Barth has interpreted Anselm's argument in a most original and interesting way. According to Barth, Anselm's argument does not really amount to a theoretical proof, to a compelling argument by means of which, for example, one could finally convince the non-believer. Rather, Anselm's proof is faith's own description of itself, a reflective presentation of that which happens in faith. It is of course a fact of human experience that there are 'fools' who 'in their hearts can say', 'There is no God' (Cf. Psalm 14: 1). If one is a fool (in the Latin text of the Psalm the word is *insipiens*, i.e., one who does not know), then this may certainly be said. If, however, he were one who knew, that is, if he knew God and if he really knew who God is, he could not on reflection say: 'There is no God'. The denial of God by the person who does not know is grounded in the fact that he does not know who God is. There are times when in this sense we are all fools. We cannot of ourselves come to a proper knowledge of *who* God is, nor can we secure for ourselves the right concept. This is something which we can only receive as a gift. But when we really understand *who* God is we are overwhelmed, and at the same time we are constrained to confess: 'Yes, God *is*.' Faith, therefore, is this right knowledge of God, and it is from this also that our 'being constrained' is derived. According to Barth's view then, this is the process which is reflected in the so-called proof of Anselm of Canterbury.

How then are we to judge these attempts to prove the existence of God? To undertake a proof of God is theologically question-able. On closer inspection it proves itself from one point of view to be impossible; and from another different standpoint to be necessary.

1. *Proofs of God in an age of 'God's eclipse'*

This is also a problem which must be faced with regard to the current problem of God, namely, the fact that in our epoch God has become question-able. (See Chapter 1.) In an age when the premiss 'God exists' was still regarded as self-evident by the greater part of society, the most obvious way for theologians to proceed was first of all to produce a proof of God as an introduction, as a purely preliminary statement, so that they could then go on to the actual subject-matter, to the real theological problems. The question of God's existence did not require lengthy discussion. For the vast majority of people this was a problem which was unquestionably settled. The proof of God's existence as an introduction to theology was employed to some extent to round off the system and to safeguard the foundation of faith against a small fringe of doubters and atheists. In our age of God's question-ability, this rather casual treatment of the question of the existence of God by means of a preliminary proof of God is no longer possible. The question whether God exists cannot be dealt with as a side-issue, nor can it be so easily settled once and for all. It is a question which arises with every theological theme; it has to be faced when we are dealing with christology, original sin, the doctrine of the church or eternal life. To put it as briefly and as clearly as possible: the *whole* of theology must be a proof of God, and theology must be 'done' as a proof of God. The method of presenting a proof of God's existence in the form of a closed argument belongs therefore to a bygone situation. In that situation it was a valid way of dealing with the question of God. However, it is no longer valid for ours.

This is one point which has to be made with regard to the historical situation. There is, however, a second: when we reflect from the standpoint of *faith*, the impossibility of proving God's existence by means of a final, closed argument becomes even more obvious. For, since faith, as encounter between *God* and *man* has these two aspects, the following question has to be dealt with from both sides, that is, with regard to God as well as in relation to the believer:

When we ourselves try to be clear about the nature of the God in whom we believe, what then becomes of the attempt to prove the existence of God by closed argument?

If the existence of God could be proved conclusively, for example in the same way as a mathematical proposition or a law of physics, or by bringing forward circumstantial evidence as in a court of law, and in such a way that no reasonable objection could be made to stand, then it would mean that God is something innerworldly, something we can encompass with our human reason and which presents itself as completely open and transparent to our minds. Understood in this way, however, God would no longer be God. He would no longer be that reality which sets limits to our minds. To speak with Anselm of Canterbury, it is precisely when we rightly understand *who* God is, that we must also understand his *in*comprehensibility.

Therefore, in view of what is implied when we use the word
'God': a God whose existence could be demonstrated by means
of a closed method of proof, like the proofs of mathematics,
would not be God. The being and nature of God makes a proof
of his existence in this sense impossible.

*What becomes of the attempt to prove the existence of God by means
of closed argument when we try to be clear about what really happens in
man's response of faith?*

That for which we can find conclusive proof can—possibly,
become a matter of indifference to us. We can say to ourselves:
'Of course, this is how it is. It is proved and cannot be doubted.
But because it is proved it does not concern me. It remains true
even when I am not concerned about it. I can therefore calmly
devote myself to other things.' In other words, a final proof
addresses itself only to the intellect; it does not speak to the
whole man, his feelings, will, and his sense of responsibility. At
least not necessarily. It is quite a different thing with regard to
the knowledge of God. For the person who genuinely accepts
the fact that God exists, such knowledge can no longer be a
matter of indifference to him. If it came to the worst, a person
could perhaps become unconcerned, but only by being wholly
and completely untrue to the essence of this knowledge. The
knowledge that God exists should lay claim to and be the
motivation of our whole existence in all its dimensions. This
means that this knowledge is a matter of response. It is gained
by risking our total existence, and cannot be settled by
theoretical proof.

But to respond, to risk one's existence in this way, is faith.
Thus faith is the only way to the knowledge of *this* reality. If we
take seriously what faith in God really means (as *knowledge*, that
God is), then theoretical, definitive proofs of God are eliminated. Faith is something total, it involves the whole person.
Proof, in the sense outlined above, is by contrast always something partial and particular. It moves exclusively on the level of
the intellect.

We spoke of the question-ability of the proof of God's existence. From one particular point of view it is regarded as impossible, from another, as necessary. We have just dealt with the question of its impossibility. But this is only one aspect of the matter, and our conclusions are valid only with regard to those proofs which are presented as closed systems of thought and which purport to offer final theoretical proof. Beside this, however, in arguments for the existence and reality of God, there is another justified and necessary factor which has to be considered. It is now our task to expound this, and in order to do so, a glance at the development in Roman Catholic theology will prove helpful.

The modern understanding of the proof of God's existence in Catholic theology

Since the time of Karl Barth and the emergence of dialectical theology there has been a marked contrast between this leading movement in Protestant theology and Catholic theology, especially with regard to proofs of the existence of God and in fact all natural theology. Catholic theology felt itself bound by the direction given by Thomas Aquinas, its normative theologian, and affirmed with him that knowledge of God was possible through the natural means of reason. Moreover, in this same connection, the First Vatican Council of 1870 decreed: 'Whoever says that the one true God, our Creator and Lord, cannot be known with certainty by means of the natural light of human reason is excommunicate' (*Doctrinal Decree on the Catholic Faith*, Chapter II, Canon 1). By contrast, from the modern Protestant point of view, it was firmly emphasised that God can be known *only through himself,* through his own sovereign act of self-revelation. (From the Old Protestant point of view, in the reformation and in Reformed and Lutheran Orthodoxy, the possibility of proofs of God's existence was something which could still be affirmed, but with one serious qualification: a person's 'natural' knowledge of God was regarded as being of no help toward personal salvation. It was therefore, practically worthless.)

However, in contemporary Catholic theology a remarkable change has taken place. We select here only one theologian who is representative of this development, Karl Rahner. Of course, the dogmatic decree of Vatican I quoted above is still adhered to: 'God can be known in the natural light of reason' (this is better rendered 'in the light of' rather than 'with the light of' because of the Latin ablative *naturali rationis lumine*, the implication being spatial rather than instrumental). On the other hand, that such basic knowledge is possible should no longer be taken to imply that a conclusive proof of the existence of God can be produced. The different proofs of God's existence are no longer understood as closed arguments or as demonstrations in the geometrical sense, but rather as different expressions of a basic experience which in principle everyone can have. It is the metaphysical experience of one's being limited and upheld by the infinite and ineffable mystery of 'being' itself. It is not necessary for man to have a clear *conception* of what this 'being' is. He simply has the *experience*. He senses that he is limited and upheld, and in the sphere of his life in the conditional, pointed toward that which is ultimately unconditional. This can happen in experiences of inspiration, in experiences of genuine love and fidelity, in the realization of transitoriness and death, in the awareness of having an inescapable moral obligation, and also in other ways. *In principle*, everyone can have this experience in his life. As a matter of fact, however, not everyone does. When a person realizes and is illuminated by such an experience then it is a gift. It is an incipient encounter with God, even when the name 'God' is not involved; it is the first tentative beginning on the way toward faith.

The different proofs of God's existence are thus forms of expressing the manifold nature of this basic experience of being directed towards the Unconditional in the midst of the conditional. This allows for the most diverse descriptions and variations. There can be no final limit to the number of 'proofs of God'.

The 'proof of God' as a dialogue about God with all men

This modern development within Catholic theology helps us to see why it is necessary to undertake proofs of God. When Thomas Aquinas concludes his different proofs of God's existence with the stereotyped remark: 'It is this (i.e., the Prime Mover, the First Cause, the Necessary Being etc.) that we call God', we are given a formula which helps us to discern the positive element with regard to proofs of God. In proofs of God's existence, faith seeks to engage in discourse about God with all men. For God is that which really concerns all men, therefore, in principle, it must be possible to enter into a dialogue about God with every man. What the word 'God' means, and what the reality of God means for human life, must not remain unintelligible. To some extent it can be settled by discussion.

We have seen of course that the reality of God can be truly known only in faith, that is, in the risk and response of the whole person. When someone is certain of God's existence and reality, this is not a theoretical certainty which could be proved by demonstration. It is a practical certainty involving personal *engagement*. The *certainty of a proof* consists in being able to regard some matter as more or less settled, and to be once and for all convinced about it. By contrast, the *certainty of faith* means a renewed and confident waiting upon God, and involves understanding, orientating and adjusting one's life accordingly. Thus the specific certainty of faith is distinguished from the other certainties which man can aquire in the world, for example, in everyday life or in science. It is not a theoretical certainty which can be obtained once and for all. It is not something which can be possessed. It is rather a practical certainty which has to be proved and tested in the action of everyday life, in our doing, our suffering, and in our total experience. For the same reasons this certainty is not oriented toward the past nor based upon knowledge gained in the past. It is a certainty directed toward the future, a certainty of *expectation*. To be certain of God in faith means to await ever anew the tokens of the divine reality. In other words, the believer experiences both the existential force of the idea of God and the appeal of God's name, and now he again awaits this experience and this confirmation, even when their form may be completely new and unexpected. His certainty lies in the fact that he cannot cease waiting upon God. However, although God can be known only in faith and in this specific certainty of faith, there is no gulf between faith and unfaith which would rule out from the start any possibility of coming to an understanding of God. Believers and non-believers are neighbours in the world. They have essentially the same human experiences. Therefore some agreement between them —at least of a tentative sort—should not in principle be impossible. However, in order to promote such understanding, the believer must address everyone else in terms of this common experience, for example, on the basis of that varied 'basic, metaphysical experience' which everyone can share. The believer must address the non-believer in terms of what he experiences in life, so that with the help of this experience he may show him how God intervenes in his life. Then he may say to him: 'This is what we call "God".' Understood in this sense, the proof of God is an event in the necessary course of the dialogue between faith and unfaith, and between faith and doubt.

The scope of this basic metaphysical experience, and the extent to which the concrete experiences of existence are comprehended and realised within it, may be expressed in the following statement drawn from contemporary Catholic theology: 'The individual has the experience of this inescapable condition of his spiritual existence . . . as the elusive, clear light of the mind, as the power given to him to question to the uttermost, a power which may be exercised in relation to himself, and which also enables him to reach radically beyond himself; in the experience of anxiety (which is not to be identified with the fear of some object), in the joy which cannot be named, in moral obligation when a person shows genuine unselfishness, in the experience of death, in which he receives an intimation of the absolute loss of all his powers. In these and in many other ways this basic, transcendental experience of human existence brings with it a disclosure of the *whole* (though we have no "vision" of it) as presence (and therefore as genuinely personal); without identifying his finite self with this basis, it is this which man experiences as the ground of his spiritual life.'[1]

This attempt to address man at the level of his basic experience and in the most diverse frontier situations of his life, the attempt to show him God in these terms is something which must be undertaken again and again. In principle, then, there can be countless proofs of God. To conclude, we may take the following statement as an example: 'Everyone can and must know that he is responsible for his life. Responsibility is a basic human experience. "Being responsible", however, is always a being responsible *before someone*, or before some court of appeal. However, when someone is responsible for *all* he says and does, then there must be some final court of appeal before which he is responsible for his life as a whole. This final court of appeal is what we call "God".' An argument such as this does not of course amount to a proof in the real sense. It could not compel the person who is not prepared to give up his doubts to believe. It is only an intimation, and as such it can serve to make one attentive. But as an intimation, it is also an element in the discussion with unfaith and with doubt. Besides, the believer must also recognize that unfaith and doubt are always to be found to some extent within the believer himself. In this sense the dialogue with unfaith is also always an inner dialogue of the believer with himself.

Proofs of God, in the way in which we have understood them to be legitimate and necessary, can therefore only to a limited degree indicate the direction in our experience of life from which we are to await God, the place toward which he can suddenly advance to meet us.

[1] Karl Rahner, Herbert Vorgrimler, *Kleines Theologisches Wörterbuch*, Art., 'Gottesbeweis.'

Chapter Four

On Being a Person

God is not known by means of proofs directed at the level of the understanding, but in an act of decision which involves the whole person: the decision of faith. Of course the understanding plays a part in this decision, but so also do will, feeling, mood and conscience. When someone chooses to believe in God, then this means that he places his entire life within this perspective. No area of life can any longer remain unaffected by this integral decision of faith. For instance, one cannot believe in God within the family circle and be an atheist in business life. It is true that some may in fact live in this way, and with regard to some particular area of life they may choose to leave God out of account. But this only shows that the faith of such a person is not yet wholly authentic and sincere. There is also the well-known example of the modern scientist who, it is suggested, must leave God behind in the cloakroom like his stick or his hat before entering his laboratory, the implication being that as far as his working method is concerned, the scientist can have nothing to do with God as a 'working hypothesis' (Bonhoeffer). For the scientist there is such a thing as a legitimate and necessary 'methodological atheism', that is to say, he must strive to solve all his problems in a purely rational way, as though there were no God. On the other hand, to the extent that he believes in God, and as a responsible person is passionately devoted to the work of research, the scientist will know that God guides him in this work and that his responsibility is a responsibility before God.

In this sense, faith lays claim to and engages the *whole person*. And for this reason, faith is rightly called a *personal act,* and in the most genuine sense a *personal decision*. And since God can be

known only through the response of the whole person in faith
it is important for our discussion of the question of God to ask
now what it really means *to be a person*.

Reciprocity

What do we mean when we say that someone is a person?
How do we know that he is a person?

In everyday life and in everyday language it would seem that
we know very well what we mean when we speak of 'persons'
and of personal relationships. On the other hand, it is by no
means easy to say what it is that decisively characterises someone as a person. What makes a person a person? Is it the fact of
being responsible, the fact that we are consciously aware of our
words and actions, that they are *our* words and actions, that we
are burdened with them and can be called to account for them?
But to this it could be objected, for example, that although a
small child or someone who is mentally ill are persons, they
cannot in any strict sense be said to be responsible. Or are we
really talking here about the *dignity of man,* 'the eternal rights of
man'? Is this what is decisive? Yet in this connection we have
to remember that there have been, perhaps are, and in
principle possibly will be again in the future, periods, societies
and cultures which pay no respect to and possibly even knew
nothing about these rights and norms of an enlightened
humanity. All this speaks for rather than against the fact that
today we regard the person, every single individual, as
responsible, as a being who possesses certain inalienable rights,
and that in our age we must do everything we possibly can to
establish this understanding of the person and of humanity
firmly in the consciousness of all mankind.

But there is something more primary, more elementary and
more essentially basic to this phenomenon of being a person;
something which we experience with the most compelling
immediacy with regard to ourselves and our fellow men, and
which evidently cannot be described simply in terms of
responsibility or of human dignity. This most basic and

primordial moment is something more simple and fundamental. It is the source and foundation of our sense of being responsible and also of the notion of human dignity.

This most basic element is apparent in *the capacity to say Thou:* to me, the other person is a thou; I am a thou to the other person. This is true for everyone. Again and again, for every human being, another person can become a thou (excepting perhaps the extreme case of the mentally ill whose personhood is somehow lost and beyond our perception). The capacity to say thou means: that I can 'address' the other in his genuine selfhood, and be 'addressed' in the same way by him; that I can give myself to him and know the experience of his giving of himself to me. This is something quite different from the mere ability to react. A slot-machine can also react, but it cannot reciprocate love or hate.

This self-giving involves *reciprocity, rapprochement, mutuality.* When I give myself to the other, address him, then I know that he knows himself to be addressed by me, and that in this situation he also addresses me. '*I* address the other as *thou;* the other is aware of this. I know, in that I address him, that the other thou also knows it.' This is the formula which helps to express the nature of this event of self-giving. It is an event which takes place only between persons, and in principle it is always possible. It can occur even when a person is not yet able to speak. An infant also experiences and reciprocates the self-giving of the mother. There appears to be only one exception to this of any interest: the possibility of 'reciprocal address' seems to be something which can be experienced between man and the more highly developed animals. This may indicate that the animal, which as far as we can judge is not in any real sense capable of speech, is nevertheless, as it were, on the threshold of being a person (Buber). For this reason it is understandable that attempts are made to establish societies for the protection of animals. It would hardly occur to anyone to establish a society for the prevention of cruelty to highly developed computers.

That man is the being who has the capacity to say 'thou' is in the last analysis also the source of the two other aspects we have mentioned: the sense of being responsible and the dignity of man. Man can be responsible because he has partners to whom he can give himself. Humanity, the worth of personhood can be claimed for a being which is capable of reciprocity. To extend humanitarian norms to include machines which can merely react, would, as we have seen, be quite meaningless. However, as we have also noted, the notion of humanity can, with some modification, be extended to include animals. Cruelty to animals rightly appears to us as inhuman. And in our technological age we must for once give serious consideration to the question whether there are not certain purely industrial methods which 'valuate' animal life (automatic chicken farms etc.!), in a way which is contrary to animal dignity and which for that reason are also inhuman!

The primal experience of being a person

We can say then that even without a philosophically worked out *concept* of personality, we basically know very well what it is to be a person. We know the reality of interpersonal relationships. We know them from within because we continually have experience of them and because we are always involved in such relationships. We know ourselves as 'I' and the other person as 'thou', and we know that the other person is an 'I' to himself just as we are a 'thou' for him. We do not have to engage in research and experiment and then infer conclusions in order to know this. We know it as a fundamental certainty, as the source of everything else. We are as certain of it as the perceptions of our five senses, possibly even more certain. It is a basic reality which cannot be seriously questioned or disputed. Ingenious proofs may be produced to convince me that the coils of my brain function in the same way as a computer. But no matter how clever such arguments may be, I know nevertheless, and will not be convinced otherwise, that I am an 'I' and not a computer. Just as I know for certain that I am an I, I know also for certain that the other, my fellow-man, is a thou and not a complex machine. These certainties, with regard both to the I and the thou are equally primal. And because of the fact that this is a matter of primal experience, *Martin Buber*, who speaks of his notion of the I-thou relationship as the 'primal reality' rightly says of his views: 'What I had to say could not be called a system . . . I could not go beyond my experience, nor did I ever wish to do so. Experience is my witness and my appeal is to experience. The experience to which I refer is naturally limited. But it is not to be understood as subjective. I have tested it through my appeal and test it again and again. To those who are listening I say: "It is your experience. Call it to mind, and whatever you cannot recall, then dare to attain it as experience".'[1]

The 'between'

It was also Martin Buber who developed the basic and most appropriate categories for all our thinking about inter-personal events, in fact for all personal occurrences and all personal reality. It would be wrong to think of persons and of personal relationships with the same categories we employ in connection with things or occurrences in the world. Either the categories somehow do not fit or some particular aspect is obscured. For a human being, a person, is not like a thing which possesses certain attributes. A person is neither a substance, nor merely the individual member of a species, nor a whole which can be reduced to its parts. Persons are not related in the same way that stones, for example, can be said to be related when they strike and move one another, or, alternatively, when they cease to do so and thus cease to be related. A person *always* exists in personal relationships and it is only within such relationships that he really *is* a person. Man cannot regard his relationships with other human beings as merely fortuitous, as something which could just as well be otherwise (like the relation between one stone and another, for example). They are essential and necessary.

[1]'Aus einer philosophischen Rechenschaft' in *Werke*, Vol. I, 1962, p. 1114.

The appropriate category for our thinking about persons and about all personal reality (for example, history), is the category of *the between*. But in this case we are not dealing merely with a category or thought-form, but with a particular phenomenon, a phenomenon of our human existence which we experience existentially.

What does Martin Buber mean by 'the between'? Man never exists alone or monologically, but always in relation with others, always socially. Such relationships can be between one person and another, between an I and a thou. It can also be a relationship to a group of people, or even to an anonymous social collective.

It has to be understood that the personal I-thou relationship should not be thought of as a relationship between two isolated individuals. We must realise that the I and the thou are always rooted in a social world. Their relationship to one another at the same time also involves a relationship to the world. I and thou cannot be conceived as subjects in abstraction from this. On the other hand, society and its conditions and structures should not be thought of as *things*, for in the end, these can be reduced to a vast number of individual relationships. The current widespread preference (also in theology) for thinking in terms of social structures is bound to appear as an abstract and unreal simplification and as finally inadequate to the demands of social and political action, especially when this simple and elementary fact is overlooked. For example, the situation of the ruler and the ruled is really actualised as a multiplicity of very diverse relationships between individuals and individual destinies. And the anonymous social forces which from time to time determine and characterise our existence as social beings are not things but people. For instance, any change in the situation between ruler and ruled and any change in social conditions takes place through individual encounters and relationships. All discussion about changing social structures which fails to take account of this fact, or which does not give it its due or take it seriously in practice, cannot lead to genuine political action and is no more than weak and empty talk. This is because, in the end, it is individuals and their decisions that really count in political action. It would be necessary to have a *hermeneutic of society* to demonstrate to what extent the basis of all social structures depends upon individuals and their encounters, their under-standing of themselves and their world. Society is not controlled by some mechanism. What happens in society, the growth and change of social structures (relationships of power, ideologies, prejudices etc.), is not determined by a mechanical process, but by the processes of the human understanding. In the last analysis, the structures of society are always shaped by the existential decisions of persons. What we have called the category of the interpersonal 'between' is that which also determines society. We must first of all accept this basic category as the presupposition and only then go on to reflect upon the emergence of what we call social structures.

The 'between' between man and man which we are con-cerned about here is something which we experience as an existential reality. This phenomenon which we constantly experience also takes on the significance of a category, of a genuine concept. This means that in the light of this simple, basic experience we can genuinely *reflect upon* the most diverse and manifold experiences of our existence. Martin Buber under-stands the 'between' as that which occurs between two or more persons. With Buber therefore, the stress is more upon the individual relationship between I and thou. However, in my view, we can and must speak of a 'between' in connection with the complex of relationships within a group consisting of more than two persons. This is because a group or a collective is constituted of a multiplicity of actual and of virtual I-thou relationships.

For example, the fact that people engage in discussion is an important phenomenon of human existence. When people are involved in a genuine discussion, then in the strict sense of the word, something takes place *between* them. Perhaps they may arrive at insights which the individual partners in the discussion could not reach by themselves. In retrospect, it is impossible to say who originated the insight, to which partner in the discussion it originally belonged, or to measure the exact contribution which each participant made so that that insight could arise. The insight is rather the result of the discussion itself. Or again, fidelity and trust are phenomena which are part of human experience. When someone trusts another, when one person is faithful to another, or when someone breaks faith or fails to trust another, in all these cases something takes place *between* the persons concerned. The same is true of every other phenomenon of our existence which is conditioned by the personal and social character of our lives—and the fact of the matter is that there is *no* phenomenon of human existence which does not have this inter-personal and social character. For example, even the undefinable anxiety which a solitary individual may experience by himself, also includes other people. For such existential anxiety always involves a hidden relationship with one's fellow-men who possibly, as far as the anxious person is concerned, may have been the cause of his disappointment, or who perhaps may have left him isolated and alone.

However, we recognize the 'between' most clearly in those interpersonal relationships which are consciously experienced as such. To attempt to assess the nature of the reciprocal experience in such a relationship (such as love, friendship, comradeship, etc.), by means of some psychologistic method,[1] which seeks simultaneously to enumerate the specific attitudes of two or more separate and isolated human subjects, is precisely to miss the phenomenon itself. It fails to grasp that which is really experienced in such a relationship. This nearest and most basic reality cannot be comprehended by means of this method. This is because the essential thing about an interpersonal relationship is the fact that the persons concerned are *mutually* affected; the

[1] By a 'psychologistic method' I understand here a way of viewing human phenomena which describes the attitudes of the human spirit not as processes of understanding but by analogy with states of affairs regarding things and the senses in which they are subject to change.

person who gives his trust, for example, and the person who receives it. In this case the one is affected by the trust of the other, and the latter also by the trustworthiness of the former. Thus it is only where *both* partners are affected that a genuine experience merges. In their being and in their 'personhood', both participants are determined, moved, changed and affected by this relational event. The essential nature of the 'between' then, is *reciprocity*. Love, for example, and even unrequited love, is always a reciprocal phenomenon. And as we have said, there is nothing whatever in human life (apart from purely physiological processes) which in some sense does not include this mutuality. Thus everything which concerns persons and everything they meet with in their history must be reflected upon with the aid of the notion of the 'between'. It is the category which is genuinely personal.

One final question must be raised: *We have been studying what it means to be a person. Is personal being only a part or a segment of reality as a whole?*

For theologians who concern themselves with the problem of what it means to be a person, this question is of fundamental importance. The problem of what it is to be a person becomes especially important in connection with the question of God, for as we have seen, God is known through personal decision and through the believer's personal giving of himself in the risk of faith. 'Personhood', then, our own being *as* persons (and not merely as biological organisms), this is the sphere in which God meets us and it is here that we recognize him. And it is as persons that we must prepare ourselves for his coming to us. But does this mean then that God has *no* dealings with nature? Does it mean that he is present only in this very small segment of reality which we call 'personhood' and 'history'? A small segment of all the millions of years, and so small as to appear quite meaningless? In other words, does this imply that God has meaning only for human history, but not for the sphere of the unhistorical or for nature?

Initially we might be inclined to say that this is so. It does look as though personal and historical reality constitutes only a very small part in a vast cosmos. But this impression is lost when we remember that our personal experience, our being persons, is the mirror in which the *whole* of reality is reflected for us, the microcosm in and through which alone the macrocosm of the whole creation is accessible to us. Even the work of the scientist, who investigates the world in an exact, experimental, impersonal and unhistorical way, is also rooted in his personal life-history. Without his personal commitment and his passionate quest for knowledge, such research, and this picture of nature which we have, would not be possible.

Therefore, when we speak of the personal, the *whole* of reality is in a certain sense at stake. A philosophical personalism which concerns itself with the special character of personal and historical existence as something to be contrasted with the scientific-technological attitude and approach to reality should not from the outset limit itself to and be determined by such a narrow basis as this. Nor should it regard this one segment of the whole of reality as its sole concern. For it could also be the case that the scientific-technological understanding of the world (the view which prevails today), does not in any sense deal with reality itself, that is, with reality as a whole, but merely with the world as it is open to partial observation. Although at this level it arrives at correct and successful results (that is, at results which are successful and effective in manipulating nature), it nevertheless cannot grasp the inner reality of individual natural phenomena. On the other hand, it may well be that 'personhood' as the microcosm in which the world is reflected to us as a whole is the means through which we are granted basic insights into the way in which the world in its essential nature can and must be understood.

The philosopher, therefore, must at least hold everything open. He should not assume from the outset that he must work solely within the confines of a personal understanding of reality. On the other hand, from the standpoint of faith, the theologian will be of the same mind as the Psalmist:

'When I look at *Thy* heavens, the work of *Thy* fingers,
    the moon and the stars which *Thou* hast established;
what is man that *Thou* art mindful of him
    and the son of man that *Thou* dost care for him?'

God is the Creator and Lord of nature and of history, and
also of the history of each individual. From his Person as the
point of reference, history and nature, the personal and the
(apparently) a-personal appear to us as a united whole.

Thus the philosopher must leave the question as to the total
character of reality open. That is to say, he must not begin with
the assumption that the seemingly a-personal sphere of nature
must be clearly distinguished from the quite different sphere of
personality and history. He must *ask* whether there may not be
some other legitimate way of viewing natural phenomena
different from the objectifying view—a way of viewing which
will relate such phenomena more closely to man as a reflecting
person, and thus at the same time 'personalize' them. The
theologian on the other hand, because of his biblical orientation
and his faith in a creator of the world, receives, so to speak, the
firm *instruction* to pose further philosophical and ontological
questions in this direction.

Chapter Five

God as Person

Faith is a personal act. It is only through the decision of the whole person that God is known. We have examined the reality of the personal and have come to the conclusion that the primary characteristic of personhood is reciprocity. Now the decision of faith is a personal act. Faith is not merely a theoretical kind of knowledge. Rather it is the practical encounter of man with God. If this is so, then more light is cast upon the reality of God, a light which can be of decisive importance for clarifying our understanding of God and which can open the way to the right concept of God. When we apply the personal categories which we discussed in the previous chapter to the personal act of faith as man's encounter with God, then we must conclude that *God is personal*. The Bible is fundamentally right when in all its parts it speaks of him in no other way. And if faith is a personal act, if reciprocity is the essence of personhood, then this reciprocity must also be of the essence of the relationship between God and man.

In the essay 'The Eclipse of God' from which we quoted in Chapter One, Martin Buber says of the word 'God': 'Where might I find a word like it to describe the highest! If I took the purest, most sparkling concept from the inner treasure-chamber of the philosophers, I could only capture thereby an unbinding product of thought. I could not capture the presence of him whom the generations of men have honoured and degraded with their awesome living and dying. I do indeed mean him whom the hell-tormented and heaven-storming generations of men mean. Certainly, they draw caricatures and write "God" underneath; they murder one another and say "in God's name". But when all madness and delusion fall to dust, when they stand over against him in the loneliest darkness and no longer say "he, he", but rather sigh "thou", shout "thou", all of them the one word, and when they then add "God", is it not the real God whom they all implore, the One Living God, the God of the children of man? Is it not he who *hears* them, who hears them with favour? And just for this reason is not the word "God", the word of appeal, the word which has become *a name*, consecrated in all human tongues for all times?"[1]

This is Buber's passionate answer to the objection that the word 'God' has become useless, that it has been desecrated by all the dreadful things that have happened among men in the name of God. It is an answer which shows how in contrast to all the philosophical concepts for the Absolute, the word 'God', as 'the word which has become a *name*', includes the Personhood of the One so named. Whoever says 'God' means *thou*. And for our purposes, the most striking thing is the exact and precise way in which Buber defines the person of God: God is a *thou;* he is 'the God of the children of man'. He is the 'One who *hears* them—who grants them a favourable hearing.' To say that God is a thou, that he is personal, means not only that as human beings we may address him; it also means that he listens. If he did not listen, our speaking to him would be an illusion. So much so that no enlightened and sensible person would have anything to do with this. But he 'hears—and hears with favour'. This means that the words we address to him are his personal concern. It is not just that we may call him 'thou' or approach him as a thou—perhaps our language can provide no better possibilities for addressing him and approaching him than this—we have to say that he really *is* a thou.

To employ this mode of argument does not mean that we thereby have some fixed conception of God. To think in this way is not to transgress the second commandment; we do not 'make an image' of God. The fact is that we are rather thinking of a particular *relationship* to God, and attempting also to clarify for ourselves the nature of that relationship. Even when a

[1] *The Eclipse of God*, pp. 17–18.

person knows that God is far greater than he can think or imagine, he still knows nevertheless that he is responsible before this God. He knows that his speaking—utterances which are not addressed to some particular person but which give expression to his life as a whole, his whole being—and his sense of responsibility, do not end in a void. He knows that they are not meaningless or in vain, but that they are, as it were, 'taken up'. This is what is meant when we apply the personal category of the 'between' and the notion of reciprocity to the relationship between man and God.

God as Person—an Anthropomorphism?

To refer to God as Person, as the Person who addresses man, who can be and wills to be addressed by man, is not to speak anthropomorphically. When the biblical witnesses, or when today, in our talk of God in preaching and in prayer, we speak about 'the finger of God', 'God's eye', 'the strong arm of God' and such like, then clearly we are using anthropomorphic expressions. Whoever does use them is usually well aware of the fact. But this is not in the same sense true with regard to the way in which the Bible speaks and thinks of God as personal. Quite the contrary. The opposite in fact would be true, for to think and speak of God as an impersonal being would be a genuine anthropomorphism! What is an anthropomorphism? Theologically speaking, it means that man conceives of God, his Creator and Lord, in terms of human forms and criteria, that he reduces the infinite to the terms of the finite.

Man creates idols for himself, idols that he can understand and grasp. He sets them up before him, but it is impossible for a genuine reciprocal relationship to exist between them. In the words of Psalm 115: 5, 6, these 'dumb idols' 'have mouths but do not speak; eyes, but do not see. They have ears, but do not hear . . .' By contrast, Psalm 94: 9 says of the true and living God, the Creator of the world: 'He who has planted the ear, does he not hear? He who formed the eye, does he not see?' And following the argument of this Psalm we must also add: he who made man a person, who made us I and thou, is he not himself also a Person, an I and a thou? He who has made man a person, and made him a partner, a person who can recognize and understand the requests and concerns of another person, does he himself not also have the capacity to recognize a personal partner, to 'care for the son of man'? (Psalm 8).

The divine reality which is of 'ultimate concern' (*Paul Tillich*) to man in his personal being must also be a personal reality. Tillich of course has also spoken of the disappearance of the 'theistic' personal God, and has further suggested that in our time, this symbol for the divine no longer has any power. The absolute faith which alone can overcome the anxiety of doubt and the threat of meaninglessness in the present, which can help modern man toward a genuine 'courage to be' (and this has been the essence of faith in all times)—this faith, according to Tillich, must hold to the 'God above God' and relinquish the God of theism. 'Theism in all its forms is transcended in the experience we have called absolute faith. It is the accepting of the acceptance without somebody or something that accepts. It is the power of being-itself that accepts and gives the courage to be . . . It cannot be described in the way the God of all forms of theism can be described . . . Only if the God of theism is transcended can the anxiety of doubt and meaninglessness be taken into the courage to be'.[1]

For Tillich, therefore, talk of God as personal, or theistic talk of God, is symbolic (and anthropomorphic). In earlier ages this way of speaking was justified and necessary. However, it can lose its power and become empty, even to the extent that it must be overcome by a new form of faith. It is precisely this, according to Tillich, which constitutes the transformation which is taking place in Christian consciousness and in the Christian form of faith.

It is interesting that in connection with this same problem regarding the question of anthropomorphism in talk of God as

[1]Paul Tillich, *The Courage to be*, pp. 179–180 (Collins, Fontana Library, London, 1962).

personal, Tillich also quotes Psalm 94 : 9 ('. . . he who has planted the ear . . . who formed the eye . . .'), and says: 'God lives in so far as he is the ground of life'.[1] And again: "Personal God" does not mean that God is *a* person. It means that God is the ground of everything personal and that he carries within himself the ontological power of personality. He is not a person, but he is not less than personal.'[2]

Tillich, in my view, is right up to a point. However, his conclusion is not quite satisfactory. As far as he goes, we must agree that if God is 'the ground of everything personal' then he himself *cannot be less than personal* and that God must live in so far as he is 'the ground of life'. And here Tillich finds support for his position in the simple and compelling argument of Psalm 94 : 9. But we must go even further: if God, as the ground of everything personal, is himself no less than personal, then in his being he cannot lack reciprocity or the 'between'. Therefore God himself, in the relationship to a personal partner such as man, must be reciprocally 'affected'. If then God is really the ground of everything personal, then this must mean that he stands over against us as 'a person', that he is the one who 'affects' us and that we 'affect' him, that he is the one who addresses us, and that he is the one addressed by us. Otherwise he also would belong with the idols 'who have eyes but do not see, who have ears but cannot hear . . .'

Thus we are in *agreement with Tillich* on this one important point, namely, that God cannot be less than personal. An a-personal or sub-personal God, and 'it', a neuter, would in fact be a man-made idol. Man would have every right to feel superior to such an idol for it is precisely the marks of person-hood that this God lacks, the distinctively human character-istics which constitute man's humanity, the power of self-giving, the 'between', reciprocity, the capacity to let the other be himself. With such a conception of God we would indeed have a real theological anthropomorphism! *Where we differ from Tillich*

[1]*Systematic Theology*, Vol. I, p. 268 (London, 1953).
[2]*Systematic Theology*, Vol. I, p. 271.

is with regard to the question whether the ground of everything personal must not logically also be *a* person.

However, with regard to another important point we must allow that Tillich is right. As 'the ground of everything personal', as the one who, for example, has constituted us as persons, God cannot simply be a person among others. The way in which he as a Person encounters us, the way in which he stands over against us as personal, is different from the way in which one human person encounters another. The difference may be provisionally expressed as follows: God is suprapersonal. Unlike ourselves, he is not a finite but an infinite Person. As infinite Person he encounters each finite person with an infinite demand and with infinite understanding. This means that in principle, two possibilities have to be considered:

a. We can think of God as an It, or as an It which is beyond every finite, innerworldly It. But even such a 'super-It' would still not be a thou.

b. We can think of God as a thou, or as a thou transcending every finite, innerworldly thou.

There seems to me to be no third possibility—or if there is, it would involve our being consistently silent about God, a resolution *not* to form any conception of him and to put him altogether beyond discussion. There are then *de facto* these alternatives: our perspective is either upon that which can understand us as persons, or it is determined by that which cannot.

To think of God as a human thou is inadequate. That is to say, such thinking would not correspond to the demand of the biblical message. Not to think of God as a thou is equally inadequate.

We have to say then that when the Bible, and when we ourselves speak anthropomorphically of God or to God in sermons, in prayer and in our theology, in expressions drawn from the sphere of human life, such as 'Father', or 'Lord', 'Judge' or 'Saviour', then we are certainly using *symbols*. And here we must also agree with Tillich again when he says that the symbol *participates* in the reality which it symbolises. They are symbols for a higher reality, a reality of which we can speak only symbolically because other linguistic means of expression are lacking. God is not just Father in the sense that the human father is a father, nor is he Judge just in the same way as a human being can be a judge. This is why words like 'Father' and 'Judge' have the character of symbols. They are not here employed in their usual, everyday sense. They point towards something which is beyond the reach of ordinary understanding. It is therefore significant when personal symbols for God, like those we have mentioned, are occasionally supplemented and corrected by a-personal symbols (such as, for instance, 'light', 'sea' or 'abyss'). These help to remind us that God is not a finite person among other finite persons. Nevertheless, personal symbols do take a certain precedence. And it is important to realise *that the 'higher reality' symbolised in personal symbols, is not an a-personal reality, but a personal reality of a higher order.*

Thus the 'thou' of our address to this infinite Person is not an inauthentic or inadequate form of speech. It is not an 'as if' (we do not use it as if it were appropriate to address God in this way). It is appropriate and it is precise. Although God is Person in this other, higher sense, he is a true and genuine thou for us, a thou who is accessible by means of the 'thou' we speak. Our 'thou' is not in vain, nor is it spoken into a void. God, the infinite Person, listens. He maintains his relationship to us in our personal needs and concerns.

God—the coming One

Even when we know God, our knowledge is never complete or final. Faith, and the knowledge of faith, are always 'on the way'. This is true of the individual believer and it is true of the different epochs and generations of the community of faith, the Church. Faith is a way. The knowledge of God is a way. And to walk in this way is to be open for that which lies before us; it involves an openness for the future.

Man's ability to comprehend is incomplete. He can never reach absolutely final conclusions. Therefore our knowledge of God can never become a closed system. It is not the kind of knowledge which we have as a secure possession and which enables us to put up inflexible and final arguments in its defence. But it is not only because of this that our knowledge of God can never be complete. It is due to the nature of God himself. It is because he is a God of history who meets us ever anew and in new ways. Exodus 3 : 14, where the *Old Testament name of God* (*Jahweh*) is interpreted 'I am that I am', or 'I shall be as I shall be', is further interpreted by Martin Buber as follows: 'JHWH (Jahweh) says, he will always be there, but always in the form in which he will then choose to be there. He who promises his presence and his support hesitates to bind himself by defining the forms of his appearance.' [1]

The understanding of God which is expressed in this interpretation of the name of God applies not only to the Old Testament, but is valid also for faith in God today. Faith is a *waiting* upon God who remains free to encounter us as he wills, in ways which are always different, and in the new events and questions of human existence and history. God determines the *epochs* of his encounters with man. Who, for example, could have foretold that the Second Vatican Council could in large measure have been responsible for initiating a transformation of Christian awareness, one which has affected every Christian believer? Faith, however, waits upon the God who is not only *free*, but who is also *faithful*, and whose promise, 'I shall be there', always holds good. Thus faith in God is a confident waiting, not a waiting in doubt and despair, and not a tired and resigned 'waiting on Godot'.

Since waiting is an essential part of faith, the future is thus the sphere from which God comes to meet us. For faith God is always the coming One. This understanding of God from the standpoint and attitude of faith does not exclude but rather includes the fact that he is also the One who is present, and

[1] From 'Moses', in Buber's *Werke*, Vol. II, p. 63.

that the past belongs to him as well. Understood in a personal way, God is the One who will be, who is, and who was. This singular inter-relationship of the three dimensions of time, which we also know from our experience of history, also exists between persons who stand in a historical relationship with one another.

For faith God can mean and can be the coming One. Another vital element in faith is also hope, waiting with confidence. This is essentially connected with the being of God as Person. That is to say, *only persons can have a future*. A stone can be there for a thousand years and yet at no point in this long time-span can it in any real sense be said to have a future. The notion of the 'future' has meaning only in the realm of the 'between', in the reciprocity between persons (see Chapter 4). In that persons have to do with one another and give themselves to one another, they are there for one another. It is only in this being with and for another that there can be any such thing as a future at all; something which comes toward man, which is not yet there but which already intimates its presence; something which can be mutually hoped for, awaited, longed for, or even feared.

The Doctrine of the Trinity

For a long time the Church and theology held that God must be thought of as personal and addressable, though not as a person in the same sense as a human being is a person. This awareness (which of course is found in the Bible in another, different form), found its articulation in the post-biblical period in the form of the doctrine of the Trinity, the doctrine of God as Three-in-One. This doctrine, along with the doctrine of the Incarnation, the doctrine that God became man, was regarded as the basic dogma of Christianity. It has no explicit basis in the Bible. It can hardly be said to be anticipated in the New Testament. It is, however, an attempt to define theologically *the* way in which the God who reveals himself in *Christ* encounters us. It is a theological attempt to define *Who He is*.

The doctrine teaches that God is of one divine substance

(divinity or 'God-hood'), in which there are three divine Persons. Now we must be careful to note that in this context the word 'person' does not have the same meaning that it has today. According to our modern understanding the word 'person' means an individual, a 'subject', possessing a consciousness of his own and distinct from other consciousnesses and individuals. According to this understanding, the doctrine of the Trinity could be interpreted in such a way as to imply that there are three divine individuals, or three Gods. This was never intended; quite the contrary, and trinitarian theology has always acted as a check upon the heresy of Tritheism, the belief in three Gods. But in addition, the ontological notion of 'substance' which is derived from the Platonic and Aristotelian philosophical tradition, has also become strange for us today. This means that we can no longer simply accept and repeat the doctrine of the Trinity in its traditional form. However, the real *intention* of the doctrine remains valid even today as a theological interpretation of the God proclaimed by Jesus.

That is to say, God is in no sense 'three Persons'. He is one Person. However, he is not a person in the sense of limited individuality, or as possessing a consciousness limited by other consciousnesses. He is of course 'personal', having 'the capacity for history', for the 'between', and for reciprocity (see Chapter 4), but he does not suffer the limitations which man suffers as a person. God therefore encounters man in his own particular way, not in the way in which one man encounters another. He comes to man as the 'Father', with the unconditional and unqualified demand of the Creator. He comes to us as the 'Son' (and here we think of the Incarnation and cross of Jesus Christ), in and through his identification with us, in his 'being for us', and through his solidarity with us which men cannot attain. And he encounters us as the Holy Spirit. This means that he can take hold of a man inwardly, inspire him and set him free in a way which is not possible among men. The difference here is not merely one of quantity or degree. To put it philosophically, it concerns the difference between the absolute and the relative: in the relativity of his own personhood, man feels himself claimed and upheld by an Absolute.

Psalm 139:2, 'thou discernest my thoughts from afar', to some extent illustrates the 'trinitarian character' of God. This exclamation indicates that God not only limits man from without but also from within. He understands man better than man understands himself. In this sense God is supremely immediate. Man is a person; he can think, feel and will. Above all, he has the capacity to communicate and to enter into relationships with others. He can address another, and be addressed by another. But man does not, as it were, have his thoughts and feelings at his own disposal. The thoughts we think and the consequences of our willing and feeling are always fragmentary. We cannot fully grasp them, nor can we see where they will lead us. We find it impossible to give them a consistent and absolutely final shape. In other words, *we do not possess our souls, they are not at our disposal.*

To say then that 'God discerns my thoughts from afar', or that, 'He limits me from within', means that even in his innermost being man cannot escape God. Even in his autonomous personhood and subjectivity he has no place to which he can withdraw. However, this does not mean that God is the absolute dictator who confines and enslaves man. The fact is that it is he alone who can make men really free. It should be clear, therefore, that the trinitarian understanding of God is not an image of God. It is not the picture of a God with human attributes who rules the world, nor of a God who returns good for good and evil for evil in accordance with some fixed code of human morality. Nor is it the invented projection of that which 'man himself is not, but desires to be' (Ludwig Feuerbach). The trinitarian understanding of God rather includes a specific *anthropology*, and from our point of view it is at this anthropological level that the truth or falsity of this understanding is decided. It is an anthropology which views man as finite, dependent (man is not at his own disposal), and incomplete. If one can understand oneself as inwardly limited in the sense in

which we have described, and if one does not simply identify
oneself with one's desires, one's different spiritual conditions
and states of consciousness, then there is room for faith in the
trinitarian God. And this faith, with its own interpretation of
the situation of human existence, may even appear inescapable.
If one does the opposite and identifies oneself with one's psychic
conditions, allowing only for the play of blind chance and
indeterminate possibilities, then basically there can be no room
for God. On this basis, of course, it would be quite consistent if
someone were to construct a 'theistic' picture of God (God as
the one who distributes rewards and punishments, for example).
He might hold firmly to this because he may think that this is
the kind of God he needs. But this picture of God is one which
rightly comes under the judgment of the critics of theistic faith.

Whatever position we adopt to this way of thinking, with its
possibilities for faith and life, this is what the ancient, basic
Christian dogma sought to express. Its intention was to answer
the question *who* God really is.

A Critique of theistic Faith

So far we have emphasised that a personal understanding of
God is indispensable. But we must also realise that a critique of
the 'theistic', that is, the personal understanding of God, is also
necessary. The Christian theologian is required to make this
effort, and in this regard he must attend to the criticisms of the
Christian church's understanding of God as personal which are
put forward by those outside the church, by those who are
critical at least of the impression which they receive. The
theologian should not only take account of this. He should also
make it fruitful for his own thinking. I should like to quote a
passage from a sermon, a passage which makes it quite clear that
such a critique is required:

'God has seen the misery of the sons of men; he has heard the
cry which has reached to heaven. Now the measure of tears
seems to be full. His mercy is now full to overflowing. The

misery in the world can wring the Son from the Father so that he must give him up. Because God could not look on any longer "the time was fulfilled" and he "sent his Son".

'But, dear friends, this is not simply God's weakness. That would be a blasphemous thought. Christmas would be the result merely of a fit of weakness on God's part. We would be thankful that he sent his Son merely because he could not have done otherwise. No, God could have acted differently; and *how* differently.

'We must not forget that it was not just misery and distress which then cried from earth to heaven. Ever since the blood of the brother Abel cried from earth to heaven it was guilt and sin, and they rose like a poisonous smoke to heaven. God has waited long. On his part this demanded unimaginable patience and restraint so that he might not give in to his mounting wrath. We must see that our guilt has all but worn God out, that our conduct has tested God's righteousness and holiness to the breaking-point . . .'

The sermon (on Galatians 4: 5, 'When the time was fulfilled, God sent his Son . . .'), from which this passage is taken does not belong to a former age but to our own. It is not the sermon of some obscure man, but of a highly respected preacher. But it seems to me that this way of speaking of God as personal is quite indefensible and cannot be taken with any seriousness. And this is only one example from many, an example of a way of speaking about God as personal which is fairly widespread among Christians. God is conceived in wholly human terms as a personal partner. His psychological reactions are described. The implication of this is that man is merely an immature child. The mystery of God vanishes, the mystery which limits and upholds man in his highest and most subtle possibilities. As far as a personal conception of God such as this is concerned, we can only agree with *Albert Einstein* when he writes:

'In the struggle for the Good, the teachers of religion must have the inner greatness to abandon the doctrine of a personal

God. They must give up all claim to that source of fear and hope from which the priests of the past have drawn such enormous power.'[1]

In connection with *this* conception of a personal God I can also agree with *Walter Bernet*, when, after quoting Einstein, he writes: 'Personalistic thinking makes possible a flight from adulthood into the illusion of a childhood-land, where reality is forgotten. The need to think transcendence consciously is transformed into the wish to trust a demanding and loving Father like a child. Personalist regression then develops like soteriology: the Father saves the child, who as a child cannot fulfil the demands of the Father's authority; he is saved from the consequences of his insufficiency. However meaningful such projections may have been in former ages with their different forms of awareness and different social structures—understood as genuine ways of thinking—they constitute a positive hindrance to man today in his attempt to overcome his present.'[2]

Today the Christian theologian must gratefully accept every critique of *this particular* understanding of God as personal. It is of little importance whether these are advanced on psychological grounds as with *Freud*, or here with Walter Bernet or whether in the name of the moral consciousness and man's moral maturity, or in the name of the evident 'moral order of the world' found in man (like Johann Gottlieb *Fichte* in the disputation about atheism). Nor can the theologian be ungrateful if such criticisms are made in the name of man's real needs, as with *Marx* and the Marxists. This critique also helps to undermine the facade of a conception of God which is shaped into an ideological construction drawn from man's superficial experience of the world. It helps us also to speak *more genuinely* of the *true* mystery of the personal God, the mystery which helps us to understand more profoundly man's situation and his experience of the world, and which also helps us to see them in a new light. However, this does not prevent certain indi-

[1] Quoted by Walter Bernet, in *Gebet*, p. 114. Kreuz Verlag, Munich, 1972.
[2] Op. cit., pp. 114f.

viduals from taking the view that the massive notion of a
personal God conceived in human terms can today still be a
valid symbol for that personal mystery.

Chapter Six

God and Jesus

I remember very clearly a discussion I once had in Rome with some colleagues who belonged to the Benedictine Order. I had put forward the thesis that as the Christian Church what we had to proclaim to men today was the one fact, namely, *that God is*, and, that properly understood, the whole Christian message in all its aspects is already contained in this one sentence. One of the Benedictines objected and asked whether the one necessary thing we had to say to the world was not Jesus Christ? In a strange way the two fronts seemed to have changed places. Would it not be more likely for the Catholic, with his long tradition of 'natural theology' to regard the existence of God as the crucial point? And should it not rather be the Protestant who regarded Jesus as decisive for Christian Faith? (We might expect this on the part of the Protestant, his background formed to some extent by Karl Barth and by the concentration of Christian thinking on Jesus Christ, or by the questions which Protestant theologians are again raising about the message of the historical Jesus.) It soon became clear to us that both of these positions had to be understood in relation to questionable tendencies in the thinking of both confessions. With regard to Catholicism, a tendency toward adopting an undifferentiated attitude and approach to the monotheistic world religions, and in Protestantism on the other hand, the tendency toward a Jesus-orientated 'post death of God theology'. The discussion finally led to the question whether in the end both confessions, with the particular points which each took to be of crucial importance, and with regard to the Church's charge to proclaim that one essential thing, were not really thinking and attempting to say *the same thing?*

But if both of these things really mean the same, how are we to think about them? How can the person who says 'God is' be saying essentially the same thing as the person who says 'Jesus of Nazareth'? That this is possible can be seen from the nature of God as Person. We can only know a person in and through our actual encounters with him. We can perceive a law of nature by its effects, and if we wish we can reproduce these effects by means of experiments. We can observe particular developments in history from the statements of the historical documents that have come down to us. But we can only know a person through personal encounter. This encounter can be direct. It can be a face to face encounter. It can also be mediated through letters or through the reports of a third party. But even in this mediated form of encounter there is an element of directness. According to the Christian confession Jesus of Nazareth is the point in history where God as Person meets us concretely and personally. It is not that we just suspect, infer, or merely have some presentiment of his presence here. This is the place where he really confronts us and addresses us. At this point he meets us not as the limiting concept of the human understanding, nor as some final theory about the world or of the moral self-understanding. The fact is that it is here that he presents himself to us as the Person he is.

Thus formulated, the question immediately arises:

Is Jesus the only point in history where God encounters us? Is God not present also in other religions?

This is an old theological question and it is one which we cannot avoid. In my view, however, the Christian answer to it must be that the Christian confession of Jesus of Nazareth is a confession to an actual event. It is not a speculation, nor is it some general theory. We have really heard God's voice through Jesus of Nazareth. In Jesus God actually encounters us and continues to encounter us. As God expresses himself in Jesus, and as he addresses us in Jesus, so God *is*. We believe that it is really with God that we have to do, and this is what we hold to.

'God' is therefore no longer some empty and obscure concept. He is a Person who has confronted us with a definite will and in a specific mode of being.

This is a real event, and for Christians the reality of this event is the determining factor. We do not set up any general dogmatic theory about this, nor do we suggest that God can *only* encounter man in this way through Jesus. On the contrary, for if God is the Lord of the world and of all mankind, then we must accept that in some way he wills to encounter all men (of all times and cultures). When our fellow-men are the object of our concern (including those who are not Christians), when we are genuinely concerned about them as *human beings* and do not forget the God in whom we believe, then we must believe that God is involved also in their destiny and in their salvation.

Due to the fact that the world religions, world views (and even religious indifference) exist in such close proximity to one another, these basically simple and existentially important reflections have recently given rise to the theological notion of *anonymous Christians*. This is a notion which was originally developed within contemporary Catholic theology. The idea of anonymous Christians was first suggested by the Jesuit Karl Rahner. However, this is a notion which is also of extreme importance for Protestants.

Moreover, although the term 'anonymous Christians' is not used, the Council has now made this part of the official teaching of the Catholic Church. The Dogmatic Constitution of Second Vatican on the doctrine of the Church states: 'Those who cannot be held guilty for not knowing the Gospel of Christ and his Church, yet who seek God with honest hearts and strive under the influence of grace to fulfil his will in its address to conscience can attain eternal salvation. Nor does divine providence deny that which is necessary to salvation to those who without guilt have not yet come to an explicit acceptance of God, yet who not without dependence upon divine grace seek to live a good life. The goodness and truth found in them is regarded by the Church as a preparation for the Gospel and as the gift of him who gives light to man that in the end he may have life.' [1]

This declaration of the Council has in view not only those who are outside the Christian faith and who belong to other religions, but also those who do not believe in a God at all ('those . . . who have not yet come to an explicit acceptance of God . . .'). Something can happen within them which can bring them to God and their salvation. It is an inward event in their conscience, an event in the depth of their existence. This takes place 'under the influence of (God's) grace,' and, 'not without dependence upon divine grace', a grace which is operative in their striving to live a good life. This inward event is not Christian faith. It is possible that it is not religious faith in any sense at all. Nevertheless, it is a reality *comparable with faith*, a movement at the most profound level of human existence which is similar to faith in God, and to Christian faith in the revelation of God in Jesus Christ. Fundamentally, it involves trust and risk, openness and love. It involves the whole man in his relationship to the ultimate and ineffable mystery of his existence. Whenever someone has this experience, when he takes this inward step not in his own strength but with the help of the grace of God which comes to him, then God encounters him. This can be so even where there is no conscious conviction of faith, and even when a man thinks he can make nothing of the word and name 'God'. For apart from an encounter with God, apart even from this hidden and concealed meeting in incognito which takes place in a hidden way amidst the everyday experiences of human life, and where the name of God appears to play no overt role, there can be no salvation for man, and his life cannot be brought to fulfilment.

One may well even go further and suggest that this experience amounts also to a hidden encounter with Jesus Christ. For whenever God chooses to have any dealings with man, when he elects him to be his partner, this happens through Jesus Christ, the Mediator between God and man: 'For there is *one* God, and

[1] Para. 16, Chapter II, in *The People of God (Das Volk Gottes)*.

there is *one* mediator between God and men, the man Christ
Jesus, who gave himself as a ransom for all' (I Tim. 2: 5). We
must also understand and interpret the non-Christian's
encounter with God in the light of Christ. And when God meets
them, he does so in the form in which he appeared in Jesus
Christ: as the One who is wholly identified with men (the
Cross!), and as the One who has opened up to man an unbounded hope and a limitless future (Easter!). In contemporary
Catholic theology, those who stand in such a hidden and
concealed relationship to God and to Christ, whose relationship
is not an obvious one and who are possibly not even aware of it,
yet who are in truth open to God, are called 'anonymous
Christians'. They do not bear the name of Christians nor do
they regard themselves as Christians, but in the reality of their
existence they are nevertheless 'something like' Christians.
They are to be found among members of other religions as well
as among unbelievers.

The Problem of the 'historical Jesus'

But these are peripheral considerations. Christians are led to
such conclusions when they think of those of their fellow-men
who are not Christians. For Christians, however, Jesus of
Nazareth is of *binding* importance. Christians confess that in
him, they encounter the Person of God. The person who as a
Christian has really understood the call of Jesus Christ will not
at the same time wish to be an anonymous Christian.

This may be formulated as follows: when we are touched by
his message, in Jesus of Nazareth we see God's *face* and recognize
his *unmistakable voice*. We may ask how this can be so. How is it
that God's encounter with a man can be so unambiguous? There
would seem to be two possibilities: either God encounters us
through the unambiguous directness of a historical personality,
or he encounters us unequivocally through some particular
teaching. When, in John's Gospel Jesus says: 'He who has seen
me has seen the Father' (14: 9), then initially it might seem to
imply either that whoever knows this historical personality

Jesus of Nazareth also knows the Father; or, it could mean that the person who does not know the personality or the character of this Jesus, but who nevertheless knows his teaching, also therefore has sufficient knowledge of the Father.

But in the case of Jesus of Nazareth, neither of these alternatives quite fits the case. And this brings us to the big theological problem of the 'historical Jesus'. In fact we have little exact historical knowledge about either the personality or the teaching of Jesus. Again and again the attempt has been made to sift the reports, to expose the genuine historical kernel and to free the personality of the historical Jesus from all the later mythical and dogmatic additions of the Christian community. But no firm conclusions with regard to this matter have ever been reached. *Albert Schweitzer's* great work, *A Quest of the Historical Jesus,* demonstrates how all the different attempts to do so came to nothing. The reason for this is that the biblical writers, to whom we are indebted for all our knowledge about Jesus of Nazareth, were evidently not interested in his historical personality or his personal development. They did not want to write a biography of a great man. They did not want to depict his character. For them, Jesus was not a historical personality. Nor was he one of the great figures in the history of the human spirit, or in the history of religion. For them, he was the Messiah promised to the people of Israel, the Son of God and the Saviour of men. What they wrote and handed down was not a faithful report about what had happened. It was primarily a confession of faith in him who after his resurrection from the dead was exalted as Lord to the right hand of his heavenly Father and present in his earthly community.

The historian of course can at least know for certain *that* Jesus of Nazareth once lived and that he died on the cross. From a historical point of view everything else with regard to detail is uncertain.

The failure of these attempts to lay bare the historical core, and the recognition that both the Evangelist John and the Apostle Paul proclaimed Christ and at the same time showed no interest in the historical Jesus, have led *Rudolf Bultmann* to the conclusion that Christian faith has nothing whatever to do with knowledge of the historical Jesus. It is enough to know *that* Jesus lived, that the content of the Christian proclamation is centred much more on the cross and resurrection, and to understand that the cross and resurrection are God's ultimate and final offer of salvation to man. According to Bultmann, the cross of Christ signifies the divine offer of a new, final, eschatological self-understanding. Man is summoned to be 'crucified with Christ,' that is, to renounce all innerworldly security, all confidence in his own accomplishments or knowledge, and to turn in total dependence toward that which comes wholly from beyond the world as a gift, toward the eschatological Word of divine promise. According to Bultmann, the resurrection of Christ means that this offer has 'cosmic dimensions', that it is valid for all men in time and history.

Against Bultmann's marked lack of theological interest in the historical Jesus, some theologians, mainly from Bultmann's own circle of pupils, have in recent years taken up the question of the historical Jesus anew. Their concern of course is not his biography or his character as a historical personality. Their concern is rather about what Jesus proclaimed, his message. And in this connection the attempt is made to separate the 'original Jesuanic' proclamation from the teaching of the earliest community, so that the original content of Jesus' preaching can be properly considered.

Here however, in my view, the results are also uncertain. Of course, when we read the Sermon on the Mount, for example (a collection of the sayings of Jesus), it can be established that Jesus evidently came with an unparalleled demand, a demand which really only God could make. In the so-called antitheses of the Sermon on the Mount, where Jesus begins, 'But I say unto you', Jesus appears as the divine interpreter and gives the authentic interpretation of the law which God gave to Moses. Or when we study the parables and other passages which report the conduct of Jesus, we see that Jesus identified himself in a quite radical way with the sinners among his people and with the outcasts of a society shaped by religion. We see that he 'claimed God on behalf of sinners' (Ernst Fuchs). These are, most probably, genuine remembrances of what Jesus of Nazareth stood for. But these fragments are still not sufficient to enable us to speak of a historically documented and definitive 'teaching of Jesus'.

When we look at all the reports about Jesus' words and deeds which have come down to us, and in particular the reports of the first three Evangelists, then we have to affirm that we can obtain neither a relatively dependable historical image of his character, nor of his religious teaching. Many individual reports have been handed down, reports about what he said or did on single occasions. From a historical point of view we do not know what really happened. We can be sure that certain elements in the reports are not historical, but are rather additions made later by the believing community ('teachings of the community') in the enthusiasm of their confession to Jesus Christ. We can also assume with certainty that, taking the Jesus-tradition of the Gospels as a whole, there are elements of genuine historical recollection which without doubt go back to Jesus himself.

This interesting and, from a historical point of view, possibly unique complex of tradition presents us therefore on the one hand with a compound of genuine historical recollection about Jesus, and on the other, with a confession to the exalted Lord and Son of God Jesus Christ whose presence is experienced in the community, and whose coming the community also awaits. There can be little historical doubt about the fact that both of these elements are to be found in the tradition. The remarkable thing about it, however, is that the line between authentic remembrance and later addition, between the historically dependable reports and the confession of faith, can no longer be drawn with any certainty. In other words, we can be absolutely sure that the Gospels report historically genuine words and deeds of Jesus, but we can no longer be sure about

which those words and deeds are. Remembrance of the earthly
Jesus and confession of the exalted Lord have so grown and
fused into a whole that we can no longer separate the one from
the other.

I must refrain here from entering into any extended discussion
of the question of the historical Jesus in modern Protestant
theology, a development which the Catholic theologian Joseph
Ratzinger has described as a 'zig-zag movement' which finds
itself poised between the dilemma of 'transposing or reducing
Christology to history on the one hand, and on the other, of
fleeing altogether from history and discarding it as superfluous
for faith.'[1] For a survey of particular problems I can recommend
here another volume of this series, Herbert Braun's *Jesus*.
For the moment I can only outline my own point of view
regarding this question. To a large extent my position is
identical with that of Martin Kähler as presented in his essay,
'The so-called historical Jesus and the historic, biblical Christ'
(1892).[2] This is an essay which in my opinion has not been
rendered out of date by the debate which has continued since
then. Kähler compared the 'historical Jesus', that is, the un-
reliable attempts to reconstruct a picture of the historical Jesus
with the *more authentic* biblical *image* of Jesus Christ. For Kähler,
the real Jesus Christ is the *efficacious* Christ, Christ as he
impressed himself upon his disciples: 'The real Christ is the
preached Christ'. This Christ we know very well, whereas with
all our attempts at historical reconstruction we never reach any
firm ground. Kähler understands the variety of New Testament
perspectives and New Testament statements about Christ as a
multiplicity of particular aspects which go to make up a
basically unitary image. In his time, Kähler could hardly have
been expected to take into account the fact not only that the
New Testament christologies vary, but also that some

[1] See his *Einführung in das Christentum*.

[2] ET Fortress Press, Philadelphia, 1964. In a shorter essay, 'The question of
the historical Jesus and the Ontology of History' (Zürich, 1960), I have taken
up Kähler's position and have attempted to bring it into relation with the
discussion about an appropriate notion of 'historical reality'.

considerable tension exists between them. But even if nowadays this is something which has to be taken more seriously, it does not necessarily count against Kähler's idea that despite particular aspectual differences, the image of the preached Christ as *a whole* remains clear and intact. As a matter of fact, Kähler's position seems to me to agree with that of the Dogmatic Constitution of the Second Vatican Council on revelation, where it says: 'After the Lord's ascension, the Apostles, *with that fuller understanding which flowed to them through their experience of Christ's glorification and from the light of the Spirit of Truth,* handed on to their hearers what he himself had said and done'.[1] (Emphasis mine.)

The relationship between both of these elements, between historical recollection about Jesus and christological confession, is so close that one can well imagine how an eye-witness, a disciple, having his own remembrances of Jesus, might see these in a new light from his position within the post-Easter Christian community. He might describe and interpret them anew in the light of this event so that to some extent his remembrance of Jesus would be transformed into a confession of faith in the Christ exalted in heaven who would come again at the end of the day. It is in this sense that Martin Buber, for example, speaks of the possibility of a 'creative experience' in his book on Moses: 'In earlier times man appropriated unplanned and unexpected events in the fundamental rapture of all the elements of his being. This is what Jakob Grimm, the great scholar of German language and literature, rightly called "objective inspiration", . . . This does not mean that what is perceived is transformed by some free flight of the imagination. The experience itself is a creative one . . . Miracle in history is not an interpretation, it is seen.'[2]

Therefore we must take the tradition about Jesus in its wholeness, as a unitary whole made up of both remembrance and confession, as a 'con-cretum' (literally, 'grown together') of

[1] Para. 19.
[2] Martin Buber, *Werke*, Vol. II, p. 17.

these combined elements which does not permit us to distil
from it either the historical personality or the historical teaching
of Jesus of Nazareth. As a concrete whole, however, the
tradition about Jesus which we possess does mediate to us a
figure, clear and unambiguous in outline. The picture provided
by the Gospels does not present us with a historical *personality*
about whom we have detailed knowledge. They confront us
rather with a definite *Person*. Whether the saying about loving
one's neighbour, or whether the Beatitudes at the beginning of
Jesus' Sermon on the Mount in Matthew's Gospel were spoken
in this form by Jesus himself or formulated in this way by the
community 'in the spirit of Jesus' is not of decisive importance.
They encounter us as a clear and radical address to our
existence. That which confronts us is not some abstract doctrine
or norm, but the address of a Person. Nor does this radical claim
encounter us in such a way that we could regard it as the
spiritual legacy of someone from the distant past. Rather,
because of the fact *that* this radical address comes to us, and
by the fact *that* we understand it, the Person who claims us in
this way *now* stands *present* and *alive* before us calling for our
response. I shall now attempt to show how we can understand
the address which is interwoven into the whole of the New
Testament as an *unambiguous* address, despite the different New
Testament images of Christ.

The One who speaks the language of God

In the claim of the New Testament preaching of Christ in
which a Person presents himself to us and lays hold of us, we
recognize the claim of God himself. For who can really command us to love our enemy (Matt. 5: 43 and par.), except he
who has created man as a person, who holds him in his hand,
and who for this reason is closer to both friend and enemy than
one friend can be to another? Apart from this assumption, the
command to love one's enemies would be sheer sentimentalism.
Or, who can command that I take no thought for tomorrow,
except he who alone has 'my times in his hand'? (Psalm 31: 15).

Without its source in him, the demand not to be anxious would only be a piece of wise psychological and medical advice. Or who could promise the kingdom to the poor in spirit, and the satisfying of those who hunger and thirst after righteousness except he who alone wholly disposes of man's life? Apart from this basis, the promise of the kingdom and the promise of ultimate satisfaction would be no more than an easy consolation about a better future, about a better life in the world to come.

Therefore we interpret the demand of Jesus, as it emerges from the tradition about him, as the demand of God himself, Lord of man's life and Lord of the world. There can be no doubt that this interpretation corresponds to Jesus' own interpretation of himself. However, in my view, if it were interpreted otherwise, its radical and binding force would be lost. As something other than the claim of the Lord of life, the call of Jesus, as far as we can still understand it today, could easily appear to be the expression of a somewhat eccentric humanism (as I have already indicated in the introduction)—and a person could have good grounds for regarding it as superior to the more balanced Socratic humanism for example, or as superior to the humanism of Jewish religion or that of the Chassidic enthusiasm for the simple man before God. But if our interpretation of the claim of Jesus is correct, then this means that God, the Lord of the world, has spoken in history, that he has spoken in human language through a concrete historical man. Jesus (whatever else one may wish to add as far as determining his relationship to God is concerned) is the One who speaks the language of God in history. And since this language is spoken, this claim expressed, then we have to say that God communicates with man.

The question however is this, namely, whether we really have to do here with an unambiguous claim, with an address which is coherent within itself, or whether the New Testament complex of tradition confronts us rather with a plurality of claims? This question becomes especially acute when we consider the insoluble compound of remembrances of Jesus and christological confession in the New Testament writings and even in each Gospel taken by itself. Do the remembrances of Jesus and the christological confessions combine in such a way as to form an unambiguous demand? That the claim which is presented throughout the whole of the New Testament is unambiguous and unmistakable, can, in my opinion, be seen from the following three points—and with this I bring the present part of our discussion to a close. The first is that Jesus is witnessed to as the Proclaimer (the One who announces God's nearness to man); secondly, as the crucified One, the One who hastens to the aid of guilty man in an act of total identification; and thirdly, as the One raised from the dead (who opens up the horizon of an unbounded future to man whose life is finite and transient). In that these three 'motifs' crystallize into one, the biblical 'image of Christ', his claim upon us is unambiguous and unmistakable. And it is this that determines the relationship of the believer to God.

Chapter Seven

Faith and Prayer

In autumn 1964, shortly before his death, I had the privilege of visiting *Martin Buber* in Jerusalem and of having a fairly long discussion with him. He told me briefly of what had happened to him on a certain occasion. For me it was the most impressive and most genuine thing I have ever heard said regarding the existence of God. Martin Buber told me: 'I met our former Prime Minister, David ben Gurion, at a reception. He asked me, "Professor Buber, why do you really believe in God?" I answered him, "If one could speak only *about* God then I would not believe either. But I believe in God because one can speak *to* him . . .".'

This episode shows how the question of the reality of God and the question concerning the possibility of prayer are inseparably bound up with one another. To speak *to* God—this is what decides the question of God, the question: does God exist? Therefore, when we reflect upon the meaning of the word 'God' and about the existence of God, we are inevitably led to the question: how is prayer possible, and what is it that happens in prayer?

Is prayer, the total dialogical attitude, an address to a court of appeal before which man's existence is wholly open and which has the capacity to hear his address? Is it an illusion, a speaking into the void, or is it a genuinely realistic act of human existence? Is prayer quite superfluous (because there is no-one there to listen)? Or, even when there is no-one there to listen, does it perhaps have a pre-eminent existential signific-ance as man's all-embracing dialogue with himself, a means of orientating and of gaining insight about his life? Or, with the help of the basic category of the 'between' (see Chapter

4) can we come to a better understanding of the phenomenon of prayer?

Prayer as man's history with God

'The eyes of faith' (Augustine) see prayer to God as an occurrence, as an event in the 'between', as a history. In whatever form they are articulated, prayers of course can only be heard and understood as the words of men. But faith dares to presuppose that these *words* constitute part of the *history* between God and man, and that consequently they are part of God's own history as well. The word of human 'response' presupposes the Word of the God who addresses man, and in its turn this response 'has an effect' upon God. One of the best examples of this are the *Psalms*. These are prayers, and as prayers, they are history. And as human history (that of an individual or a group) they are also God's history. Take, for instance, Psalm 139: 'O Lord, thou hast searched me and known me! Thou knowest when I sit down and when I rise up; thou discernest my thoughts from afar . . .' There is nothing forced about this. It looks like no more than a man's private meditation upon God. And yet, from the standpoint of faith, something happens between God and the worshipper; in prayer, the worshipper 'realizes' God, and this God encounters him. Special mention is made of this intervention of God in the intimate history described in the 73rd Psalm. It deals with the prosperity of the wicked and the misery of the pious, and with the lonely despair of the worshipper who, like Job, has to come to terms with this same problem. Then in verses 16ff. we read: 'But when I thought how to understand this, it seemed to me a wearisome task, *until I went into the sanctuary of God,* then I perceived their end. Truly thou dost set them in slippery places; thou dost make them fall to ruin . . .' In an interpretation, Martin Buber has described the decisive moment of this Psalm (indicated in the phrase, 'until I went into the sanctuary of God') as follows: 'Here he (the worshipper) receives a revelation of "constancy". He who approaches the mystery with an open heart knows that he is constantly with God. It is a revelation. To imagine that this is simply a matter of pious feeling would be to fail to grasp this experience in its wholeness. With man there is no constancy, only with God. The Psalmist has experienced the fact that God and he himself are constantly together'.[1]

In his prayer, the worshipper 'realizes' himself and God, and because this takes place, a history happens *between* him and God. We may consider this remarkable fact further with reference to the text of a prayer written by Thomas Aquinas. It reads as follows: 'Give me, O Lord, a heart that is watchful, that no rash thought may separate me from thee; a noble heart, that no unworthy feeling can degrade; an upright heart, that no equivocal purpose can cause me to stray from the way; a heart that is strong and which no hardship can break; a heart that is free and enslaved to no passion. Give me, O Lord, understanding, that I may know thee; a zeal which seeks thee; the wisdom that finds thee; a life which pleaseth thee; a perseverance which holds to thee with confidence, and the trust which possesses thee at the end.' The thought of this text is extremely condensed, and to do it proper justice one would really have to interpret each phrase in turn. However, it is in the genuine sense address, and not just in a formal sense (because it is in the second person). The one who prays opens himself for God, he bears himself up toward God and exposes his whole life before him. He does this without enumerating any of the particular characteristics of his past or present life. He does this, to take an image, in that he casts his future into God. Before God, he proves himself to be in need, he appears as one who could be separated from God by a rash thought, degraded by unworthy feeling, who could be led astray by a doubtful purpose, who could be broken by hardship and enslaved by passion. This is he. This is his confession. Yet at the same time, he is not this man, for he prays for a heart that is watchful, noble, upright, strong and free. In opening himself wholly to God, the

[1] Martin Buber, *Werke,* Vol. II, pp. 978f.

worshipper longs to receive himself from God. God stands
between the self that he lays before him and the self that he
desires, between his 'old' and his 'new' (or future) heart.

We must note carefully, however, that the man who makes
this request and this confession, and the heart which with God's
help he will receive, is *one and the same man*. The fact that God
is 'between', that he to some extent is the 'between' who
determines man's life, does not mean that man thereby becomes
a divided self. God rather enables a man precisely to be a self,
to be himself. The fact is that man can only receive himself as
a gift. This is how he stands in relation to God. And in this
prayer, this is what is confessed. In this sense man does not
stand before God as a self-sufficient person. It is rather that as
a self, in a man's own particular selfhood, he is wholly upheld
by and wholly dependent upon God. It is difficult to picture
this relationship. It is all-embracing and unique and there is
nothing else in our experience quite like it. We cannot make
this relationship between God and man more concrete by
comparing it with something similar or more familiar. We grasp
it only in its actual realization. This is precisely what happens
in prayer.

This can be pointedly formulated as follows: the 'between'
between God and man is unique. It consists in the fact that God
at once stands between man's self and his (future) self, so that
man owes his self wholly to God. This never happens between
man and man.

Faith presupposes that God hears prayer—that he 'listens
and grants a favourable hearing' (Buber), to the man who prays.
If God did not hear prayer, there would be no 'between'.

Man speaks and God hears. This means that something
happens *between* them, something takes place in man's self and in
his heart. But this also has an effect upon God himself. Whenever I really hear, I am somehow affected. Whenever I really
hear a question which is directed at me (I could also *over*hear
it above a din), something happens to me; I become the one
who is challenged to give an answer. This is so even when I

have resolved to be silent and not to answer the question. But even then I am still involved with the question, and I involve myself even when I am determined to be silent.

But God is not silent. He hears, and he hears with favour. Here we may recall the saying of Jesus in the Sermon on the Mount (Matt. 7 : 7) : 'Ask, and it will be given you; seek, and you will find; knock, and it will be opened unto you.' With regard to this promise of Jesus, we can say that the meaning of the Word become flesh and of the revelation of God in Jesus Christ is that *this* is how it stands between God and man; that God listens and does not keep silent, that he hears, and hears with favour. To this extent, the words of our prayers are not just words; they are an event of human existence, an event in a 'between'. It is not that man speaks into a void, or that nothing happens. In the depth of man's existence and in the depth of his 'heart' something does happen which finds its expression and which comes to speech in prayer.

But the depth of existence, the innermost place of the heart, is not a place to which man can wholly withdraw so that at last he can be alone with himself. It is rather the place where he exists *coram Deo* (before God). And because he exists in the 'between' before God, and is at the same time wholly indebted to God for his selfhood, because God listens and grants him a favourable hearing, this event in the innermost depth of man's heart which finds expression in the prayer for a heart that is watchful, noble, strong and free, is a way of man's being before and with God. The person who prays in this way—not just with his lips, but with the innermost part of his being, *receives* in prayer the heart for which he asks. With God, and with his help and 'sympathy', he already advances to meet that future for which he prays. He advances to receive the new heart which God will give him. His prayer is already a step toward that for which he prays. And this will be proved to him in future moments of his life. No rash thought will separate him from God, no passion will enslave him . . . His prayer, this movement in the depth of his heart, will be authenticated step by step in his life. It will embrace and integrate his life.

We can now grasp *what it is that really happens in prayer. Prayer is an event which God himself always sets in motion. It also 'affects' him, for it is his will that man should seek and find him.*

What we have done here is to offer a brief interpretation of a particular prayer—an interpretation which seeks not so much to answer the question, What does it mean?—for with this question prayer as prayer is not really grasped. Rather, we have begun to ask, What it is that *happens* when a prayer like this is made? In dealing with this of course, we have adopted a particular presupposition, the presupposition which is made by the worshipper himself, namely, that God hears him, that there is One there who listens, for otherwise, he would not pray at all. However, it may be that by making this assumption, we gain a most subtle insight into man's essential being and are thus enabled to express it. It may be that when we think of man in this way, as in his innermost being existing toward God in the 'between', we also have the best and most satisfactory way of giving expression to who man is, and of expressing who we ourselves are.

Petitionary prayer

We must now take a further step. A new aspect of prayer is disclosed when in its content and intention it reaches beyond the limits of the individual's history with God. This is *prayer as petition*. In the Bible this is quite a familiar phenomenon. I do not see how proper justice can be done to all the different parts of Scripture if this is not taken into account. But as theologians, we must also try to *understand* this familiar form of prayer.

We begin to grasp it when we give up the customary individualistic notion of man. Much more than we think, our lives are ultimately bound up with the lives of other people. Their history is our history; our history is their history. *Dietrich Bonhoeffer* gave vigorous expression to this when he wrote from prison: 'It is only then that we feel how closely our own lives are bound up with other people's, and in fact how the centre of our own lives is outside ourselves, and how little we are separate entities. The "as though it were a part of me" is perfectly true, as I have often felt after hearing that one of my colleagues or pupils had been killed. I think it is a literal fact of nature that human life extends far beyond our physical existence.'[1]

In order to understand that prayer for others is meaningful (once our individualistic understanding of man has finally been overcome), does not at all imply that we must accept the notion of supernatural, incomprehensible, divine intervention. Just as I myself can be aware of having a history before and with God, so I can also understand that together with others I also have a history before God. But the depth and solidarity of this relationship with others has to be understood as mediated by God. Therefore, I can and I should call upon God on behalf of the other. Everything depends on whether I dare to recognize and accept the 'between' between God and man. There is nothing self-evident about this. It is the risk of faith. There is no need for more miracle. There is simply the wonder of God's constant presence with men. This is what is involved when, for example, I call upon God to strengthen the faith of another person and to increase his knowledge of God. I have the firm expectation that God will do this. This is what we find, for instance in the apostolic letters. Take the letter to the Colossians, for example, where we read: '. . . we have not ceased to pray for you, asking that you may be filled with the knowledge of his will in all spiritual wisdom and understanding, to lead a life worthy of the Lord, fully pleasing to him, bearing fruit in every good work and increasing in the knowledge of God' (Col. 1: 9ff.).

Therefore, in order to come to a basic understanding of the significance of petitionary prayer, we are not required to make a study of psychological and para-psychological observations such as suggestion and telepathy and so on. These areas are still largely unresearched, and the extent to which we in fact have anything to do with them is still by no means clear. However,

[1] *Letters and Papers from Prison*, p. 65 (Letter of 5.9.43).

concerning the problem of Christian petitionary prayer, we are not here concerned with the working of some mysterious forces of nature, but with the most appropriate way in which we can comprehend something which is part of our everyday experience, namely, the fundamental solidarity of human life.

God's presence in the whole of Reality

But we must take yet a further step. For our purposes, we can take a biblical story as the model. After his dream at Bethel, Jacob prays to the Lord: 'If God will be with me, and will keep me in this way that I go, and will give me bread to eat and clothing to wear, so that I come again to my father's house in peace, then the Lord shall be my God' (Genesis 28: 20–21). And returning after some years, he prays: 'I am not worthy of the least of all the steadfast love and all the faithfulness which thou hast shown to thy servant, for with only my staff I crossed this Jordan; and now I have become two companies. Deliver me, I pray thee, from the hand of my brother, from the hand of Esau . . .' (Genesis 32: 10–11). These requests and thanksgivings are not spoken with regard to his own inner development before God. It rather involves a total context. Everything that a man can be concerned about is included in this dialogue of requesting and receiving, of question and answer with God. Jacob's first prayer takes the archaic form of a vow. Although this form has become strange to us, it can at least be pointed out that here, in the form of a kind of treaty, it is assumed that an actual transaction takes place between God and the worshipper, an invisible yet real event which has a bearing upon the whole network of relationships within a man's entire world.

In their converse with God, this is the assumption which over the centuries all Christians have made. But in order to understand it, we must try to avoid 'thinking in two spheres', a way of thinking which Dietrich Bonhoeffer so resolutely opposed, but which due to the 'closed immanence' (the idea that the world runs like a machine) of the 'modern world view' is again being urged upon the theologian today. The Christian thinker today might at first feel tempted to accept this modern world view and to regard as valid the closed immanence which goes along with it. Over and above this he then posits the existence of another quite different and even separate sphere, namely, the sphere of 'existential decisions'. This becomes the 'upper storey'.

Nevertheless, if we take the view that this two-storey understanding of reality is to be avoided, then neither can theology avoid the basic task of *ontological* reflection, that is, reflection about the essential nature of all reality. One objective task in this connection is to give proper place to the mathematical and statistical conception of reality (we have a great deal to learn from the methodological reflections of the scientist himself), to recognize it as a useful and effective abstraction, but to realize also that every secular world view is a kind of myth which we should in no sense attempt to justify with the help of Christian slogans.

The following remarks are meant to indicate the direction in which such ontological reflection should go. Behind all our encounters, there is *the personal depth of all reality*. This is how Martin Buber tells of the Chassidic Rabbi Levi Jizchak von Berditschew: 'The Rabbi used to sing a song which went as follows:

"Wherever I go—thou! wherever I stand—thou!
Only thou, again thou, always thou!
Thou, thou, thou!
When it goes well with me—thou! When I am in pain—
thou!
Only thou, again thou, always thou!
Thou, thou, thou!
Heaven—thou, Earth—thou, above—thou, below—thou,
Wherever I go, in every extremity
Only thou, again thou, always thou!
Thou, thou, thou!" '

This enthusiastic song is an expression of the way in which

the divine, the eternal thou is present in all reality. In this respect man's dealings with reality become a dialogue. Of course man's dealing with reality is also technological and manipulative. But in relation to the dialogical approach this attitude is only a partial one—or at least ought to be. In this technological age there is the threat that the technological and manipulative approach to reality may be absolutized thus rendering man's life illusory and leading him to imagine that to master reality is to know it.

The model which helps us to discover the nature of reality as a whole is the model of dialogue; not that of a dead mechanical process, nor that of the solitary decision of the individual. It is not quite enough to define the historicity of human existence, the reality of man's life in and with the world, in terms of the responsibility of the individual. 'To exist historically' certainly means to exist as a responsible subject. But responsibility is not the only defining characteristic. It is true that as persons we are always responsible, but we are not responsible for everything. It is precisely at the point where we reach the limit of our responsibility that we may discover meaning. The dialogical I-thou model helps to express the two sides of this matter: on the one hand, we are always called to be responsible, but on the other, meaning, and all that we receive, come to us from beyond our responsibility. In this sense, prayer, the dialogue *which excludes nothing*, can become our guide to the understanding of reality. Prayer is a universal dialogue; a dialogue which includes everything that concerns our existence as a whole and everything that touches upon our lives. In this way it differs from the particular dialogues in which we engage with other individual human partners.

To accept this personal understanding of the world as a whole is not to rationalize or to ontologize reality. It does not relieve us of the decision of faith, but is rather faith's own reflective expression of itself. In a single moment the whole world discloses itself anew in God's light to the eye of faith. This is what happens when prayer breaks through to the personal depth of reality. This is something we can experience, but it never becomes our secure possession. We are not relieved of the risk of faith, nor of committing ourselves totally. It can happen that the light that lightens everything can suddenly appear to us. *Dietrich Bonhoeffer* once described this breaking through to the personal depth of reality as follows: '. . . God (meets) us no longer as "thou", but also disguised in the "It"; so in the last resort my question is how we are to find the "Thou" in this "It" (i.e., "fate"), or, in other words, how does "fate" really become "guidance"?'[1]

[1] *Letters and Papers from Prison*, pp. 133–134 (Letter of 21.2.1944).

Chapter Eight

The post-theistic Critique of the dialogical Understanding of Prayer

A post-theistic theology which has departed from the biblical and traditional understanding of God as personal, is required to come to terms with the problem of prayer. It is self-evident that the understanding of prayer which we have developed here (prayer as an event in the 'between' between personal partners), is not acceptable to this kind of theology. But as a religious and Christian phenomenon prayer is something which cannot be denied or overlooked. This theology is therefore required to develop a meaningful conception of prayer, a conception however, which is quite different from the notion of prayer as address to a divine thou. This it has doubtless achieved, for this theology has also sketched out a meaningful and expressive picture of what prayer is meant to be. But the question remains whether the biblical and traditional understanding of prayer as dialogue does not contain essential elements of meaning (and possibly therefore of truth as well) which this post-theistic conception of prayer has been forced to discard.

In what follows I shall deal mainly with the work of *Gert Otto*, a representative of post-theistic theology who in his book *Reason* (*Vernunft*, Volume 5 of the series 'Theological Themes'), has devoted a separate chapter to 'The Transformation of Prayer'. Otto's basic thesis on prayer runs as follows: 'Rational faith understands prayer as identical with the quest for a responsible form of life. It involves a renunciation of that thoughtless prayer which gives itself a metaphysical dispensation from the need to be responsible for the world.'

Here we may also include the first two theses of the 'Political Vigil in Cologne'[1] which correspond exactly with this position:

[1] *Politisches Nachtgebet in Köln*, Eds. Sölle and Steffensky, 1969, p. 24.

1. Christian prayer renounces miracle; it seeks no magical transformation of the situation.

2. Prayer prepares man to take over responsibility for his world. The activity of God does not replace the activity of man.

This enlightened conception of prayer clearly has a *positive side* to it: prayer should not exempt us from responsibility. It should rather indicate where our responsibility lies and heighten our sense of responsibility. It also has a *negative side:* the appeal to a divine thou in the expectation of a miracle, of an intervention in the continuum of reality serves only to grant that metaphysical dispensation from concrete responsibility for the world. Thus prayer, understood in the traditional sense as a dialogue with the God who rules the world, and understood as petition, is unrealistic in an age of the enlightened spirit. On the other hand, prayer, as a meditative dialogue with oneself which helps to heighten one's sense of responsibility is appropriate to reality. For prayer should never be a substitute for concrete, responsible action. This helps to explain the post-theistic theologians' special liking (e.g., Gert Otto in the book cited here, and Dorothee Sölle) for a particular passage in Bertolt Brecht's *Mother Courage and her Children*. The mute, Kattrin, by resolute action manages to save the city of Halle which is threatened by imperial troops, but in so doing she loses her life. This happens while the peasants, in their anxiety about the fate of the city, hold stubbornly to the idea that they are helpless and can do nothing to save the city except pray. Kattrin, concludes Gert Otto, 'took over, as it were, the "function" of the God who did not intervene.'[1]

Walter Bernet's post-theistic interpretation of the phenomenon of prayer lays less emphasis upon action and upon the acceptance of concrete responsibility for the world.[2] For him, prayer is man's meditation and reflection upon the dimension of 'mystery' inherent in every experience. However, it is certainly not clear to me how this mystery of experience is to be under-

[1]Op. cit., p. 99.
[2]See his *Gebet (Prayer)*, Kreuz Verlag, Munich, 1972.

stood. By comparison, Otto's and D. Sölle's definition of prayer
as a sharpening of conscience appears much more clearly
defined. (It should be noted that for D. Sölle, this definition of
prayer is not exhaustive.)

I should now like to give a brief outline of the way in which
Gert Otto arrives at his conception of prayer, especially with
reference to the New Testament witness. Otto recognizes of
course that address to the divine thou and expectation of divine
intervention form an essential part of the New Testament
understanding of prayer. However, according to Otto, these
particular conceptions belong generally to late antiquity; they
are not specifically Christian and must therefore be discarded.
'Such ideas are bound up with intellectual presuppositions
which without exception are no longer ours' (p. 87). Otto
obviously has a very clear idea of what 'reality' can mean and
what it can not, also of what are and are not our specific
intellectual assumptions. 'Though it happens frequently, it is
impossible when one takes a historical-critical approach to
Scripture to exclude, for example, the notion of miracle, and
yet at the same time to retain an anachronistic, unhistorical and
pre-critical attitude to prayer' (p. 87). At the basis of Otto's
view is the concept of *enlightenment*. And it is in the chapter on
prayer that we detect traces of the ontological naiveté of the
enlightener: one simply knows. To man, reality is essentially
transparent. To this extent he has 'come of age' and bears full
responsibility for the world. There is no point in raising any
new metaphysical question about the essential nature of reality.
Walter Bernet, on the other hand, still retains at least some
indication, however undefined, that all experience has a
'dimension of mystery', a notion which he develops in connection with his understanding of prayer.

Alongside this 'late-ancient' personalism and belief in
miracle, Otto discovers another series of statements which are
integral to the New Testament understanding of prayer. 'These
are found throughout the whole of the New Testament and are
summed up in the phrase: "Pray without ceasing" ' (p. 88).

' "Pray without ceasing" means: Live your whole life in that attitude which corresponds to the attitude of prayer. Prayer as an individual act will then cease to be meaningful or important' (p. 89).

This is a considerable statement. But then he goes on to draw a contrast. He is right of course when he says: 'Whoever calls upon us to pray ceaselessly, cannot mean that we should constantly be uttering prayers' (p. 88). Yet for Otto, prayer as an individual act and as a cultic performance involves address to the divine thou and also the expectation of divine interventions. By contrast, prayer as 'praying without ceasing' goes hand in hand with monological meditation about one's responsibility in the world. He accuses Luther of retreating behind the new and radical understanding of prayer because of his attempt to combine the two. (See pp. 91f.) However, neither does Otto give sufficient consideration to the relationship between individual act and basic attitude in general, nor does it occur to him to consider whether the notion of 'praying without ceasing' could not itself be fundamentally *dialogical in character,* as implying a constant and conscious existing before the face of an infinite thou (not, that is, as implying the constant speaking of prayers, but as signifying the radical nature of 'dialogical existence'). It would be difficult to dispute that this is the way in which it is understood in the New Testament. And it is certainly difficult to understand why a modern theologian should not give this possibility any serious consideration.

In my view, it is this premature contrast which demonstrates the decisive weakness of this post-theistic understanding of prayer. Those who adopt this view have been unable to grasp the fact that the basic attitude of human existence is dialogical, and that man can exist toward an 'inclusive' and infinite thou. It may well be that this is what is understood existentially (I would not dispute this; there are some passages in the work of Dorothee Sölle, for example, when she speaks of the 'surplus of questions and of hope', which strongly confirm it), but it is not worked out *conceptually.* It receives no systematic theological treatment. But this is precisely what is required if one is concerned not to depart thoughtlessly from one of (if not *the*) basic ideas of the biblical and Christian tradition, and if one is to avoid being manoeuvred into a theological cul-de-sac.

Apart from Gert Otto, the work of *Dorothee Sölle* also suffers from this lack of sustained systematic thinking. She writes (in some respects rightly and well):

'A short time ago I asked an author why he read the newspaper every morning. He answered that reading the newspaper was something like having morning prayers, something which earlier generations used to have. He said that one sought reassurance about the total situation. I wondered whether this "total situation" was another word for God—or, if Christ were alive today, whether he would have read the newspapers instead of praying . . . To participate in the total situation—also in weakness and in resignation—belongs wholly within this context of our readiness for and our questions about transcendence, questions which have their basis precisely in the excess, in our strength, and therefore in the corresponding ability to stand up to frustrations.' [1]

Prayer does, of course, involve a relationship to the total situation, to the total situation of one's own existence as well as to the total situation which includes those things (people, states of affairs, things) which are in some sense matters of concern for the worshipper. Nevertheless, reading the newspaper cannot simply be a *substitute for* prayer (although prayer could take this form). For prayer, as distinct from merely reading the newspaper, is a *dialogue* about the total situation. It draws the total situation into a dialogue. It can, and often does take place in such a way that we are not always aware of it; it remains undefined. But this is how it usually happens. In prayer, a new dialogical dimension is added to our experience, to our reflection about experience and about the total situation. This means that in reflecting about the total situation I am

[1] *Atheistisch an Gott glauben*, 1968, p. 89.

confronted not just with myself, with other people, conditions and things, nor merely with chance or the thought of unrealized possibilities. Rather, I find myself confronted with the inclusive and infinite thou. This not I; it stands over against me. Unlike chance, and unlike possibilities not yet realized, it is not ambiguous. And although it cannot be objectively described, it is definitive. Thus it is the source of the call which comes to me to bear responsibility. Unlike particulars—people, conditions or things—I cannot evade it. It is inescapable. And this is what we understand by 'God' ('. . . *quod omnes nominant Deum*', cf. Chapter 3)—and this is what we 'realize' in prayer.

Lastly, I must now examine some of the points made by a fellow-countryman of mine, *Walter Bernet*. Bernet is also among those who give no consideration to the possibility of radical dialogical existence. In one of his chapters in his study on prayer he discusses the inaugural lecture which I gave in Basel, 'Theology as Prayer and as a Science'.[1] There I put forward the thesis that just as every (*non a priori*) science has its basis in certain experiences, so theology also has its basis in the (quite specific) experience of prayer. I argued that it was not enough simply to take the texts of the Bible as the basis for theology for these can also be studied and read from a purely 'neutral' religious-historical point of view. I cannot discuss the real core of Bernet's criticism here. I can only give some indication of how he has understood me in one (possibly the most important) particular respect. He writes:

'Must then theology give up its claim to be scientific? By no means! Faith only retreats from experience when it is not engaged in prayer. When faith is, as it were, taken up into prayer, it connects with experience' (p. 55).

This is how Bernet has understood and summarised my argument. He evidently means that for me, prayer is some kind of special experience which attaches itself to faith and which thus suddenly supplies the experiential basis which faith had

[1] In *Theologische Zeitschrift*, 1958, 14, pp. 120ff.

hitherto lacked. Prayer, as he interprets my position, is a special experience among others. This of course was not what I meant. What I meant was that faith and prayer coincide. The view I took was that faith is at the same time always prayer. Faith is a total dialogical attitude; prayer is the realization of universal, inclusive dialogue, of the dialogue which in principle embraces the whole life of the believer—'Pray without ceasing!' For the believer, this dialogical dimension penetrates everything he experiences; it penetrates the total situation. This is the specific and yet at the same time comprehensive experience of the believer, and it is in this experience that the reflective thinking of theology has its foundation. This does not mean that the dialogue just wanders aimlessly; it is guided by a concrete content, namely, the way in which God has expressed himself in Jesus Christ. (See the Chapter on 'God and Jesus'.) *This* is the partner in the dialogue.

As far as I can see, none of these post-theistic theologians has discussed the notion of total dialogical existence in the sense of Paul's 'pray without ceasing'[1] (a text upon which I think I have more right to base my case than they), because they have failed to deal with the question of the *ontological order* of personality. For personhood, understood as involving reciprocity, is the basic characteristic of what it means to be human, and it is the fundamental mode in which we experience reality. (See the Chapter 'On being a Person'.) Thus for them, prayer as a turning toward the eternal thou, as appeal, thanksgiving, as an expression of grief or of praise, can only be a peculiar individual action which is no longer appropriate to the current conception of reality. They are not prepared to consider that this can be a continuous, meaningful and genuine basic mode of existence.

Further, when one excludes from the start the possibility that man's essential situation is dialogical in character, that whether consciously aware of it or not his life is constantly guided (and even saturated) by the infinite thou of his existence, then to

[1] I Thess. 5:17.

expect a divine response or a divine 'intervention' must of course appear as an inferior and naive kind of 'miracle-faith', and as a cowardly self-exemption from concrete responsibility in the world. But against this we must say that the visible realm of man's life is surrounded by another invisible sphere of existence which is not at his disposal. That one should call upon God in the expectation that he will act out of this invisible sphere, so that his action will be effective in our life and in the lives of other, is at least a possibility in life which can be made meaningful and genuine. This can be illustrated by a simple example: Imagine that I share in an encounter with others. The situation threatens to become difficult and it looks as though it will end in quarrels and misunderstanding. Let us also imagine that in this situation I ask God to send his Spirit, the Spirit of community and of understanding. It can so happen that my attitude will change; I suddenly become aware that I am not my own master and that other people are not their own masters either. Thus I enter the situation in the expectation that one possibility may still be open, that there is still a chance that God the Father, the One who sets all men free, will be present, that he will guide and inwardly determine our hearts and provide us with new motives. In this way I may be enabled to meet the other in greater openness and freedom. And possibly, to my astonishment, I shall meet with that same freedom and openness in the other. God is then in our midst. God is, as it were, the space in which our freedom is realized. We approach one another in him. And suddenly, there is a future where there was none before, a solution where hitherto there had been no way out. In this way my prayer has changed things.

Of course this straightforward situation which we have described here can be interpreted in other ways. Someone who does not assume the existence of a personal God, who rejects the dialogical notion of prayer, could interpret it as the coincidence of a set of fortuitous but favourable circumstances accidentally creating a situation of good will. Nevertheless, the interpretation given here describes reflections as well as existential attitudes which are meaningful and genuine. It presupposes a point of view which is perhaps of more value than just hoping to chance. It can give man more freedom and more inward courage to rally his will and to concentrate on the essential task. Above all, it treats the heart of the matter with all seriousness in the sense that it is presupposed that man is not at his own disposal (and this is not *only* because his freedom is limited by the freedom of others), that *he is more than he is*. (See also the conclusion to our final chapter 'The Difference'.)

It should now be quite clear that prayer, as address to a thou and as the expectation of a divine response, by no means conflicts with concrete responsibility in and for the world. Understood in this sense, prayer and responsibility are not mutually exclusive but intimately bound up with one another. To this Dietrich Bonhoeffer testifies, for example, in his notes 'On the Sovereignty of God in History' ('. . . who waits for and answers sincere prayers and responsible actions . . .'), and also with his strong emphasis upon the kind of responsible action exemplified in his own life. Only insincere prayer can be a substitute for action, not dialogical prayer as such! This is where the post-theistic theology of prayer falls short. It seems to have failed to understand Bonhoeffer's dialectic of 'resistance' and 'submission' and the relationship between prayer and responsibility which this implies. Or has it perhaps grasped this? The last of the seven theses adopted at the 'Political Vigil in Cologne' runs as follows:

'Even when a man can no longer be helped by other men, and when he himself can no longer act, prayer keeps alive his hunger for the Kingdom of God, makes him more human in that he refuses to succumb to resignation, and does not permit him to despair of the world's meaning'.

We would have to give further consideration to the possible meaning of this statement. But without actually expressing it, it may be that it has theistic implications.

Chapter Nine

How can we speak of God?

If we wish to accept Martin Buber's statement quoted at the beginning of Chapter 7, that he believed in God not because God can be spoken *about,* but because he can be spoken *to*—how then can we still speak 'about' God? We speak about him continually, not only in theological books and lectures, but in sermons and in the work of pastoral care. It happens whenever we speak a word of comfort or reprimand to another with reference to God in the name of God.

Or should we not rather regard this as an impossible and inadmissible enterprise? As a preacher and pastor, this is one of the questions to which Karl Barth gave such serious consideration, and in fact it is this question which lays the foundation of his theological work. He writes: 'God does not belong to the world. Therefore he does not belong to the series of objects for which we have categories and words by means of which we draw the attention of others to them, and bring them into relation with them. Of God it is impossible to speak, because he is neither a natural nor a spiritual object. If we *speak* of him, we are no longer speaking of *him*.'[1] And earlier still in his *The Word of God and the Word of Man:* 'As theologians we ought to speak of God. We are human, however, and so cannot speak of God. We ought therefore to recognize both our obligation and our inability and by that very recognition give God the glory. This is our perplexity. The rest of our task fades into insignificance by comparison.'[2] Barth's solution is that in our own strength and with our own possibilities it is impossible for *us* to speak of God. The fact that we speak about him and yet

[1] *Church Dogmatics,* Vol. I, part 2, p. 750.
[2] *The Word of God and the Word of Man,* London, 1928, p. 186.

are unable to do so is a fault which God *himself* forgives, and in doing so he takes our human words and concepts which in themselves are inappropriate and transforms them into a fitting witness to himself.

Troubled by the same problem, Rudolf Bultmann has also wrestled with this question. In his essay, 'What does it mean to speak of God?' he writes: 'If "speaking of God" is understood as "speaking about God", then such speaking has no meaning whatever, for its subject, God, is lost in the very moment it takes place. Whenever the idea, God, comes to mind, it connotes that God is the Almighty; in other words, God is the reality determining all else. But this idea is not recognized at all when I speak *about* God, i.e., when I regard God as an object of thought, about which I can inform myself if I take a standpoint . . .'[1] This then is Bultmann's solution: of God, that is, about God as an object we simply cannot speak. We know nothing 'objective' about God, nothing with regard to what God is 'in himself'. Our knowledge of him is thus different from what we can know about things in the world. But we understand full well what God means for human existence in the decision of faith, what his significance is for the life of the believer, or, in other words: we know what he does to man. Therefore, to speak properly of *God*, we must speak of *human existence*, the existence of that person for whom God means something through faith.

In the twenties, the most decisive years for theology in this century, this is how two such different thinkers as Karl Barth and Rudolf Bultmann had nevertheless the same radical experience of God's 'wholly otherness', of God as God. In the same way, both of them came up against the major problem: how can we speak of God at all? If God is really *God*, and not merely a human concept or idea, how are we to speak of him? The answers of both of these theologians to this basic problem are of course characteristically quite different.

But this is by no means a new problem in theology. It has

[1]*Faith and Understanding*, Vol. I, p. 53 (SCM Press, 1969).

always troubled the Christian thinker. The question has arisen again and again: how can the language of man the creature apply to the Creator himself? In the history of theology there have been different solutions to this problem. It has been argued, for example, that we can speak of God and his attributes only in a negative way, by denying him the attributes of the creature: he can *not* be thought of in spatial terms, he is *in*-finite, *im*-mortal, *in*-visible, and so on. But apart from this 'negative way' (*via negativa*), it was also proposed that if one is really to have access to God and describe him, then the predicates of human speech must be *raised* to the level of the infinite: God is *omni*-potent, *omni*-scient, *all* good and *all* wise and so on (*via eminentiae*). Finally, in order to deal with the problems, the concept of *analogy* (correspondence) was employed. For instance, when we use a human word (such as the word 'Father', or the word 'wisdom', or the word 'power'), with reference to God and with reference to the creature, a thing or a person, the word does not have exactly the same meaning in both cases. When we call God 'wise', for example, then we must know that he cannot be wise in the same sense as a human being can be wise, that his wisdom is of another kind. But on the other hand, we also know that when the word 'wise' is applied both to God and to man, the meanings cannot be totally different, as though the word 'wise' in the one statement had nothing more to do with and nothing more in common with the word 'wise' in the other. Then it would certainly be quite meaningless to say that God is wise or that he is anything else. Despite the difference there must nevertheless be a certain analogy or correspondence between the word as used in one statement (e.g., 'Socrates is wise'), and the word as employed in the other (e.g., 'God is wise').

This problem is unavoidable. However, in my opinion, there is a much simpler and clearer answer than the traditional solutions (negative way, way of eminence, analogy), and than those offered by either Barth or Bultmann. The answer which I have in mind is not simply a rejection of the different solutions we have just outlined. But its starting-point seems to me to be simpler, more fundamental and thus more plausible. My answer is based, namely, on Buber's statement that although we cannot speak *about* God, we can nevertheless speak *to* him. Man, the man who believes in God (for only he wishes to speak of God— the unbeliever will at best speak only about a concept of God, a God who in his opinion does not exist!), stands in a *dialogical relationship* to God, in an I-thou relationship. Of God he cannot say 'he'; least of all can he say 'it'. He can only say 'thou'. It is impossible for him then to speak *of* God or *about* God.

But he does in fact speak about God, especially when he speaks to another person. Thus he certainly does want to make statements about God. He says: 'God is this, God is such.' He wants to communicate something about God to the other person. From time to time Martin Buber also, it would appear, speaks about God.

But by itself, this can be misleading: no-one can give a report on God to another, he cannot present him with inform-ation about God. One cannot break out of the dialogical relationship to God or out of the I-thou relationship thus making God, as it were, a third person, a subject for discussion. All we can do is this: we can only attempt to bring the other person into the dialogical relationship to God. We can appeal to him so that he also may begin to speak *to* God of his own account.

The dialogue thus is not abandoned. But instead of it taking place between two persons, the worshipper and God, it is now extended to include three or more, God, the worshipper and his fellow-partners. That God's presence is neither visible nor audible, and that he does not intervene, does not at all alter the basic dialogical character of the total situation. When someone wishes to help the other understand God, he does not speak as though God were an absent third person or some neutral matter of fact about which one could inform oneself. Such a person, in his speaking to the other about God, will himself at the same time remain expectantly open toward God.

He speaks silently and indirectly also to God *in* his speaking to the other person, so that God may disclose himself to him again in his Spirit, and grant both the speaker and the person to whom he is speaking a deeper understanding of what he is trying to say.

When we leaf through the pages of the Psalter, Christianity's oldest prayer book, we find Psalms which speak *to* God in the second person, and some which appear to speak *about* him in the third person. There is also a good number of Psalms in which God is referred to sometimes as 'he' and sometimes as 'thou'. For example, Psalm 27:1:

> 'The Lord is my light and my salvation;
>   whom shall I fear?
> The Lord is the stronghold of my life;
>   of whom shall I be afraid?

And verses 7 and 8:

> Hear, O Lord, when I cry aloud,
>   be gracious to me and answer me!
> Thou hast said, "Seek ye my face."
>   My heart says to thee,
> "Thy face, O Lord, do I seek." '

However, in line with what we have just said, the 'he' is really a disguised 'thou'. The believer, the person who is meditating upon God, while he may seem to be speaking about God in the third person, is not in the least suggesting that he can make statements about God in the same way that he can make statements about an object.

How then can we speak *to God*? If God is so different from all creation, how can human speech relate to him in the form of the second person and in the form of address? Why is it that, according to Buber's statement, although we cannot speak *about* God, we can nevertheless 'speak *to* him'? The answer is that it is because God is the initiator of the relationship between man and himself, and because God addresses us and 'means' us. It is God who creates the relationship of partnership. Christian faith is aware of this relationship of partnership because it knows itself to be addressed by God in Christ. Being addressed in this way *is* in fact partnership. And that this partnership exists between God and man, that it in fact happens and that God really is our 'Father', forms the content of the Christ-event. The believer does not think that he knows something about God or that he can inform others about God. Nevertheless, he addresses God out of the depth and breadth of his existence. Thus the only really adequate form of human speech which relates to God is prayer.

However, when there is any discussion about God among believers, or between believers and non-believers, then in this case also the 'he' which refers to God must remain, as in the Psalms, a disguised 'thou', and whatever the believer says must retain its basis in prayer. When I say, for example, 'God is omnipotent', or, 'God is omniscient', it *only seems* that I am making an objective statement about God. What I really mean is: 'Thou God, canst do all things', and, 'Thou God, knowest all things'. Take again Psalm 139. To put it in blunt, dogmatic terms it is saying 'God is omniscient'.—

> Thou searchest out my path and my lying down,
> and art acquainted with all my ways.
> Even before a word is on my tongue,
> lo, O Lord, thou knowest it altogether. (*verses 3 and 4*).

That plain, dogmatic statement is only an abbreviation for what this Psalm is really saying. It bespeaks the perspective of one's whole existence, of God's countenance lifted upon and illuminating our lives, of our existence in the light of the divine thou.

Finally, when a believer says to another person: 'God is omniscient', he does not mean: 'Allow me to inform you that God is omniscient'. His intention, based upon experience and upon his hope in life, is rather to say: 'This is also a possibility for you! You yourself can try (and you have reason to do so) to understand and find meaning for your life in this way.' And at the same time he is speaking silently within himself: 'Lord, who knowest all our ways and all our thoughts, grant that the person to whom I speak and I also, may truly understand our lives in thy light!'

As I have already said, I am not asserting that the other solutions to this extremely difficult question about how man can speak of God (the solutions offered by Barth, Bultmann, with the help of analogy etc.) are wrong. I am only suggesting that everything could be simpler and more illuminating if it were treated in terms of prayer, for this is the real heart of the matter.

Chapter Ten

The Difference
(On the practical consequences of faith in God)

One of Bertolt Brecht's 'Stories about Herr Keuner' runs as follows: 'Someone once asked Herr K. if there was a God. Herr K. said: "My advice to you is to think whether your conduct would change in accordance with the answer to that question. If it did not change then the question could be set aside. If it were to change, then I could help you at least by saying, you have already decided: You need a God." '

This is where I should like to begin. For it seems to me that Brecht is absolutely right. For if man's conduct does not change in accordance with the answer he gives to the question of God, if it makes no practical difference to him, then the question is of no consequence. It can be calmly set aside. I once heard a Marxist philosopher declare: 'In the end, it could well be that there is a God. But we know nothing at all about him. The question is therefore of no importance whatever. It has no influence whatever upon our lives.'

But if we agree that Bertolt Brecht (or Herr K.) is right, then we must understand the word 'conduct' not only in the narrow sense of outward, visible behaviour, but in a deeper sense as comprehending man's deeper spiritual and intellectual life as well. There is also such a thing as *inward conduct*. It can happen that something may change in a man's inner conduct, in his attitude to existence as a whole. Only later, step by step, does this change in his conduct become *visible* to and observable by others.

Thus in all our reflections about God we are finally faced with the one practical question: What real difference does it make whether a person believes in God or not?

In what way can the believer be distinguished from others? What is it that is different in the lives of those who believe in God? If no satisfactory answer can be found, then all that has been said above collapses and becomes meaningless. Or at least it will all remain in the balance until someone who knows can supply a satisfactory answer to the question of the difference it makes.

Forgiveness, Hope, Freedom

What is the life of the person who believes in God like? Or, more precisely, how can he, and in what sense is he obliged to live a life that corresponds to his faith? In dealing with this question we shall concentrate on Christian faith in God. Our concern here is not with other forms of monotheistic religion. Those of other religions who believe in one God must speak for themselves in this regard. It is their task to say what God means for them and how they understand him.

I would describe the Christian mode of existence or the Christian 'life-style' as it were, as a *life in the freedom of* forgiveness. As one who believes in God, the Christian can forgive his fellow-men and he can also forgive himself. He can do this because he believes that he is himself forgiven. He holds with confidence and with certainty to the fifth petition of the Lord's Prayer: 'Forgive us our debts as we forgive our debtors.' He prays these words in the certain knowledge that he will receive a favourable hearing. This of course is bound up with the Christian's belief that God has irrevocably identified himself with man in the cross of Jesus Christ. However, as we have already stated, the whole of Christian faith can be summed up in the one statement: 'God is'. This has to be rightly understood. God is—and this God who is, who addresses us and whom we address, is, according to the understanding of Christian faith (the faith which hears God's voice in Jesus of Nazareth), a God who wants to encounter us in *this* way, through his radical solidarity with man and with the offer of unlimited forgiveness. He who as a Christian says: 'God is', has already said that which includes everything else. It includes the coming of Jesus Christ, Christ's cross and resurrection, the forgiveness which God offers to man, and the hope which through Christ is made available to man.

But in practical terms what does it mean to live life in the freedom of forgiveness? Man is the being who seeks and has need of meaning. Human existence bears within itself the *will* that it should be meaningful. The question remains open whether this is a meaning which man creates for himself and which he gives to his life, or whether it is a meaning which comes from beyond himself and which he receives as a gift. The richest experience of meaning which man can share is in his relationships with other people, in love and in loyalty, in the readiness for self-sacrifice and in trust.

Man, however, as the one who seeks and has a need for meaning, is also the being who is poised over the abyss of meaninglessness and constantly threatened with the loss of meaning. For man, existence can become meaningless and empty. The threat of futility and nothingness constantly hangs over him. The suffering which I cause another because of carelessness and indifference, vanity and vindictiveness, the wounds which I inflict upon the other mean that for him life loses its meaning— but when I find myself in the position in which I can see the whole situation clearly, I discover that because of this I have also suffered the same loss! My life can also suffer a loss of meaning, for example, because of the aimless and useless way in which I squander my time, because I waste time in cowardly hesitation or in worrying myself about empty cares and so many other things.

However, this loss of meaning is not just some misfortune that happens to befall us, nor some tragic fate which hangs over us. It is bound up with the fact that we are responsible persons. This means that man experiences the loss of meaning as *guilt*, as his own guilt or as that of others, but most often as a mixture of both. The guilt which I incur because of the nothingness of my existence is what the Bible and Christian doctrine call *sin*. Everyone is a sinner in that the guilt which he incurs because of the nothingness of his life constitutes a threat to him, and because in a certain sense it always catches up with him.

Life in the freedom of forgiveness means the overcoming of this self-incurred meaninglessness. It means that a man can become free from the burden of the past with its wounds and its emptiness, and that freed from this burden he can face the future. This deliverance is not confined:

1. To a single occasion; it is not simply a once-for-all amnesty, but happens ever anew, and

2. because of the way in which men's destinies are so closely bound up with one another, it is not confined to the individual but includes his fellow-men as well. If it did not hold for both, if it did not extend to both, then it would not be a genuine deliverance. The person who lives in this forgiveness has the freedom to make a new beginning for himself and with others. There is basically no limit to the number of times he can begin anew. (Thus Jesus says to Peter that he should forgive his brother 'seventy times seven'—(Matt. 18: 21-22.) A man may regret past guilt and make expiation for it. But the past must not cling to him like a burden from which he cannot set himself free. And in addition to this: not only with regard to himself, but also in relation to his fellow-men, the man who lives from forgiveness has the freedom, the flexibility, the distance and the humour of a person who can make new beginnings and who can grant new opportunities to others. And in that he does not take things tragically, he also has the capacity to let his neighbour be free.

How does a person find this freedom? The forgiveness which I grant as well as that which I receive, the attitude of confidence in the other and of confidence in myself, the inner freedom of being ready to forgive and so to create an atmosphere of freedom in which I and others can breathe—I can create none of these things by myself. This freedom of forgiveness is not the arbitrary invention of the man who is a law unto himself. There is no natural necessity about it, nor is it grounded in any human necessity to provide a morality for the protection of society.

Society can be satisfied with a principle of justice. It has no place for the notion of forgiveness. Even conscience, our awareness of being responsible, can by no means make forgiveness a necessity. A principle of fitting expiation can also suffice for the moral conscience. Nor, finally, is the forgiveness of guilt a mere forgetting, that with the process of time everything will gradually be forgotten. It is rather a genuine pronouncement of acquittal: 'Freedom is something which can only be *called* forth, in that one must literally "pronounce" the other free. This means to speak in such a way that one "passes" freedom to the other, allowing the other to take his stance within the freedom which is offered to him.'[1]

Forgiveness presupposes that there is a person there who forgives. Life in the freedom of forgiveness and faith in God thus belong together. The fifth petition of the Lord's Prayer is therefore quite decisive with regard to the whole question of the reality of God. For a man is empowered to live in the freedom of forgiveness when he knows that the existence of the one who is guilty before him (his 'debtor'), and his own guilt-laden life as well, are nevertheless both accepted at the level of the same higher court of appeal. And this higher court of appeal can be none other than he who created them and who is the Lord of both. Paul Tillich's notion of 'absolute faith' as 'the accepting of the acceptance without somebody or something that accepts'[2] leads us into complete obscurity. It is meaningless to speak of 'acceptance' apart from someone who accepts. We no longer know what we are talking about, so much so that it would be better to follow Ludwig Wittgenstein's principle that: 'Whereof one cannot speak, thereof one must be silent'. On the other hand, *the accepting of acceptance,* the acceptance of the other as well as my acceptance of myself, is a reality. It is a genuine attitude. We encounter people who really hold this attitude, and this is where the *difference* lies.

Much the same is also true of *hope*. A Christian who lives

[1] Gerhard Ebeling, *Gott und Wort,* p. 49.
[2] *The Courage to be,* pp. 179–180; see also Chapter 5.

as his faith in God demands never gives up hope. For him there can be no such thing as a totally hopeless situation in life. There is always hope for others as well as for himself. Some of a man's hopes can come to nothing, but never *the* hope which concerns his life as a whole. Thus the believer firmly hopes for himself and for others even when in human terms there seems to be nothing left to hope for, and even when he himself no longer has any motive for hoping which can be measured according to everyday, this-wordly understanding. This can hold good in situations in life when the most extreme boundary is reached, when only death (or nothingness, as far as ordinary, everyday understanding is concerned) remains. And it also has a 'this-wordly' validity in that it enables one to continue to hope for the person who in human terms must be regarded as a 'hopeless case'. The poems of Kurt Marti, the Swiss pastor and poet, are a witness to Christian faith. In the volume *Funeral Orations*, he writes of such a 'hopeless case' as follows:

> 'there was never any lack of people
> who tried to show him the better way
> no-one needs to reproach himself
>
> but he shunned his counsellors and his rescuers on purpose
> and mostly chose the worse—
> or what we call the worse
>
> the question for us is whether
> perhaps for him
> the worse was the better?'

For a person to continue to hope in a hopeless situation could also be a sign of cowardice. One can easily shut one's eyes to the real hopelessness of a situation. Or it can simply be the mark of a sanguine and irrepressibly optimistic temperament. But both of these explanations would be totally rejected by the believer. For him, the motive for his hope lies with God. Even in apparently hopeless situations he knows that his life and the life of his fellow-men are hidden with God, the Creator and Lord of their lives.

This of course is bound up with the Christian's hope of the resurrection of the dead and of eternal life. And this indicates that faith in God and in eternal life are not two different dogmas or doctrines. They presuppose the one single perspective. Faith in God is the point upon which everything else depends. God is man's future and his hope, not just on the other side of death, but already in this life. The decisive thing is that it is *he* who is man's hope.

This again points to a difference in attitude, a difference which consequently must be seen to affect outward conduct. For hope implies *inventiveness*. The person who still hopes, passionately seeks and finds the ways and means which will enable him to continue to live a meaningful life. He endeavours to improve the situation for himself and for others, and to restore it to order. This does not mean of course that the non-believer cannot express such imagination, or that he cannot have the same spirit of inventiveness. It does mean, however, that the person who believes in God has a constraining motive for exercising his powers of invention and imagination. This is because he knows that he has to do with God, not only in those boundary situations, where, judged in human terms, there is nothing left to hope for, but in every possible situation. He is convinced that no situation is ever closed. To the eyes of faith there is always room—not merely for the play of empty possibility or for blind fate—but for the presence of God, the God who is concerned to restore order and who awaits man's creative and inventive action. Because God is present, the believer thus meets the changing situations of life in an attitude of ultimate and inexpressible optimism, an optimism which is not conditioned by temperament.

Just as the believer's life of freedom in forgiveness is shown to be grounded in God's solidarity with man in the cross of Christ, so his life of hope in the gift of God's future is grounded in the resurrection of Jesus Christ from the dead. Thus the cross and resurrection, the two most important 'facts of salvation' of New Testament faith are the *ways and the modes in which God himself wants to encounter men.* They are not merely facts of salvation in the sense of events which happened in the past and which can be plotted on a salvation-historical line. No, they are much more the fundamental mark and demonstration of the way in which God stands in relation to men.

Finally, faith in God, properly understood, sets man free for *responsible and courageous action.* As such it is quite the opposite of a *laisser faire* attitude. Nor is it an opium of the people offering some cheap comfort for the beyond. In certain circumstances the over-scrupulous person may never manage to act at all because he feels that there is always the chance that he may do something which he ought not to do. Does this mean then that the field of action, the determining of events, must be left to the unscrupulous with his lack of responsibility? Must the courage to act be linked with an element of unscrupulousness? Genuine courage for conscious and responsible action is rather something which belongs to the person who knows that no man finally holds the issue of things in his hands, and that his own human and imperfect action is hidden with and accepted by the One who does control the issues of life. This peculiar combination of activity and passivity, of the human action and the hiddenness of that action in God (of resistance and submission) in the attitude of the man who finds his true freedom in faith has often been described by Dietrich Bonhoeffer. The following two verses of his poem 'Stations on the Road to Freedom' are an example:

Action
Daring to do what is right, not what fancy may tell you,
    valiantly grasping occasions, not cravenly doubting—
    freedom comes only through deeds, not through
    thoughts taking wing.

Faint not nor fear, but go out to the storm and the action,
    trusting in God whose commandment you faithfully
    follow; freedom, exultant, will welcome your spirit
    with joy.

Suffering

A change has come indeed. Your hands, so strong and
  active, are bound; in helplessness now you see your
  action is ended; you sigh in relief, your cause
  committing to stronger hands; so now you may rest
  contented.

Only for one blissful moment could you draw near to
  touch freedom; then, that it might be perfected in
  glory, you gave it to God.[1]

Bonhoeffer wrote these lines in prison on the 21st of July
1944, shortly before news was received of the failure of the
attempt on Hitler's life. For him, this was the moment when
'resistance' had to become 'submission'. He had already
reflected upon the relationship between these attitudes (see
Letters and Papers from Prison, pp. 133–134, Letter of 21.2.1944).
The fact is that resistance, that is, my own resolute action, is
already bound up with submission to the God who is ready to
forgive and who gives me the courage for resolute action.

Is it necessary to use the word 'God'?

So then there is indeed a difference to be seen in the conduct
of the person who believes in God; a difference at least which is
apparent in the attitudes of those who truly seek to live out the
implications of their faith. There are of course those who do not
do this and who are inconsistent. We are concerned, however,
with those who are.

Further aspects could of course be taken into consideration in
addition to the three we have mentioned:

1. Life in the freedom of forgiveness;
2. the power to hope in every situation;
3. the courage to act responsibly.

But these three aspects are sufficient as helping us to deal with
our problem. The question is now whether the same conduct
cannot be found in the person who has no use for the word 'God',
and who does not believe in God. This is a question to which

[1]*Letters and Papers from Prison*, 1967, p. 203 (Letter of 21.7.1944).

we have to give some consideration, for we do in fact encounter such people. Does this not mean then that the difference is obliterated? Does it mean that faith in God again becomes irrelevant?

Some might object as follows: 'When people who do not believe in God display the same attitudes, then we have to say that they cannot really be the same attitudes at all because they clearly act from different motives. If they are prepared to forgive themselves and others then this is due only to their forbearance and good nature. If their life is informed by hope, then this can only be a sign of their innate optimism. Even their readiness for decisive action is simply a mark of their temperament.' But this sort of explanation is hardly fair. It would amount to a somewhat unjustified, improper and disreputable attempt to rescue faith in God, and our convictions, to impute motives less worthy than our own to those who do not share these convictions.

If we are not prepared to adopt this approach then we must allow that the motives of those who do not believe in God, yet whose conduct is like that of believers, cannot be due merely to the nature of their temperament. Where else do we find the motive? For any motive which can be compared with that which is implied by faith and upon which an existential attitude like this could be based we look and search in vain. The attachment to some ideal of humanity, for example, cannot possibly provide that ineffable hope which implies that no situation is ever closed, nor can it provide room for a person to act. Thus we are faced with the odd fact, or the possibility, that although people like this indeed *have* a motive for their conduct, they do not *know* what that motive is and are not expressly aware of it. Seen in *this* way, the situation is then not so inconceivable or strange, for we can understand that God, as the Creator and Lord of life, is close to all men in incognito and in a hidden way. He can be near to man and can encounter him hidden in the events, the human encounters and the questions of man's daily life. We have already referred to this possibility in our discussion about 'anonymous Christians' in Chapter 6. In the light of these considerations this conclusion is one which we can hardly avoid.

Thus we may conclude that *the motivation of the person who does not believe in God, yet whose conduct is like that of a person who really does believe in God, is given by none other than God himself who has encountered him in a hidden way.* Therefore the difference which it makes when one believes in God remains. We could say then that on the basis of his experience of a hidden and anonymous experience of God, the conduct of the non-believer can be the same as that of the believer. But the person who does believe nevertheless has an open and clear motive for adopting *this* attitude! One may appeal to him through this constraining motive which he has consciously accepted for himself. In terms of this motive he is answerable to others and to himself.

However, we can examine this question in another form: Could not the motive for this attitude be such as to exclude any reference to God? Could it not be determined simply by the human situation, the 'condition humane'? Could the difference which we have attempted to describe still not be a meaningful one even when the word 'God' is omitted? Could it not still be meaningful apart from presupposing the existence of the highest reality signified by this word? Is not Bertolt Brecht right when in the second part of his story about Herr K. he says: 'If your conduct were to change, then I could help you at least by saying, you have already decided: You need a God'? That is to say, you need the notion of God to give expression to a motive which *we* also have, but which we can express without this idea!

Thus the word 'God', the notion also of a real God, would be no more than a cipher used by some people to justify their conduct to themselves to the extent that it is in accordance with this. I almost have the impression that this is the view taken by *Herbert Braun* when he writes: 'The reader may ask: "Is it not then a question of the word 'God'?" Yes, he has understood this correctly. The word itself is not important. It is much more a matter of the attitude of the person who is called to obedience, and who knows that although he is unworthy, he nevertheless receives the power to be genuinely obedient. It is a matter therefore of *that* attitude which in the Jesus-tradition came under the heading of the term "God", which men received as a gift and a task. The need for the word "God" is not one of the distinctive characteristics of this attitude.'[1]

Why should it then be necessary to speak of God at all nowadays? Should we not simply speak of man, since it is among men that everything is decided, and everything judged at the bar of human conduct? Or must we speak of God just because the Bible and the Jesus-tradition compel us to do so, merely because we, as a matter of fact, relate our Christian talk of God to a tradition which once used this cipher, this word 'God'? By itself, this does not provide us with sufficient grounds for speaking of God today, especially when the same thing can be said in another way!

One thing we must consider, however, is the fact that the word 'God', as grasped and as understood by faith, is not just a word like other words. It is rather the 'Word of address', the 'Word which has become a name' (Martin Buber, cf. Chapter 4). Whoever regards this word merely as a cipher for a human attitude or an interhuman event, as a cipher which can be forgone or if necessary eliminated so that the whole question is left unaffected, forgets or excludes an entire dimension. *The dimension which is forgotten or eliminated is precisely the dimension of 'address', of the dialogical relationship between God and man, the dimension of prayer, and of the 'between' in the relationship of persons to their Creator.*

The characteristics which are exclusive to the attitude of the believer and which make his conduct different are closely bound up with this dimension of address. It is from the thou that I address that I receive the gifts of forgiveness and freedom. From nowhere else can I receive the boundless hope or the safety in which my decisions have to be made. These are all existential

[1] *Jesus*, pp. 169f. (Theological Themes, Vol. 1, 1969. Trans. note: page ref. here refers to German ed.).

experiences in the daily life of the believer and of his fellow-men. They can be tested and they can be shown to be *genuine* experiences. But divorced from this 'dialogical dimension', without this broad horizon or heaven, and viewed apart from the reality of a life lived wholly in the light of the thou whom we may address, they collapse and lose all content and meaning. For this reason, faith cannot renounce the word 'God'. It cannot cease to think about the One signified by this word. It is not a question of the mere word, the three letters which make up the word 'God'. This we could forgo, as did the pious Jew when he refused to speak the name of God. The word itself can be replaced by 'Father' or 'Lord', or simply 'thou'. What is of decisive importance and cannot be abandoned is the word of address as such. What really counts is the address itself and the One to whom that address is made.

Freedom, the forgiveness of guilt (that is, release from the burden of my past), hope, as the open future which I cannot of my own powers create, and the fact that my actions are safely hidden with a God who is not at my disposal, who takes my actions up into himself and who is more than 'blind chance'— this presupposes a special openness of human existence. It is not the kind of openness which consists in not knowing what man will become. This would be an ambiguous and even negative kind of openness. The real experiences we refer to are granted to man. He can have these experiences as long as it is assumed that man can be open to receive something positive *in addition* to what he is (freedom, hope, the courage to act), things which are not within his own control. That sphere which is not at man's disposal, the sphere by which his life is controlled, becomes accessible through the word of address, through the word 'thou', and as long as the word is not addressed to a particular individual but to the whole horizon of existence, it is also made accessible through the name 'God'. For 'thou' means everything that is beyond 'I'. And although the 'thou' is never at my disposal it is not some void or empty negation but something entirely positive.

God and the problem of being human in a technological age

What we have been saying about the practical differences which faith makes may sound individualistic. We have spoken about the freedom of forgiveness, the forgiveness in which we encounter our neighbour as an individual. We have referred to a boundless hope—the question of hope in the particular situation of the individual, and we have spoken also about the decisions which the individual has to make.

Nevertheless, it would be wrong to regard this as individualistic. However, in bringing our discussion to a close, we must now deal with the consequences which faith in God has with regard to society. We cannot of course examine this problem in general terms. We must begin with the actual situation in and for which we ourselves share responsibility. The situation is that of man on the way toward the year 2000.

In dealing with the ever-broadening, total and unitary nature of technological world-society it will not be necessary for our purposes to examine each particular futurological perspective in turn. Through technology, however, possibilities for inhumanity have grown to monstrous proportions. Not only life in general, but human and personal life is threatened to the extent that it may become part of the technological machine. According to Paul Schütz, the most monstrous and threatening of the revolutions which are at hand and which has already begun, is the biochemical revolution. His excellent book, *Why I am not yet a Christian*[1], contains descriptions of the satanic situation of man left to himself and with complete control of himself, the future of man as it confronts us. We can mention these only in passing. With the help of the 'parable of the lost Father', Schütz describes the situation of 'man alone in the world' in the 'new era without God'. He presents a picture of man 'who for the first time in the history of this earth faces no-one but himself':

> 'There was a father who had two sons. He left them and
> went to a far country.

[1] *Warum ich noch nicht ein Christ bin,* Third Ed., 1969.

Enemies carried war into the sons' land. Their property was burned to the ground. Their wives were violated. They themselves were beaten half to death.

But they stood up again, rebuilt their house and began life anew from the ruins. It was not to the lost father that they turned to seek meaning. Both he and the meaning were lost forever. Things had no meaning. The only meaning there could be was the meaning they themselves could give to things. And so they slaughtered a calf for the foundation-laying and were happy that things were better than before.'

Schütz remarks: 'This is what it will certainly come to in world history. Both of these parables will be weighed in the balance; the parable of the lost son[1], and the parable of the lost father. There is little more to say. This is how things stand today. History will weigh it out. And it will be weighed out with blood, shrieks and tears. Not with books and manifestoes. Up to the last breath. Without mercy . . . Who was truly lost, the father or the son? . . .'

If man himself has biological control over his fellow-man, if he himself in his organic and psychic being can become part of the technology at his disposal—who then is there to stop him?

As soon as these possibilities become clearer to a greater number of people then it is understandable that a wave of protest should surge across the world. This is entirely necessary and perhaps also one of the few great hopes of our own age. Generations to come want to remain human. In its broadest impulse there is certainly a revolution aimed at achieving humanity. Nevertheless, the question again arises as to who it is that establishes the criteria of humanity?

Aldous Huxley's terrifying vision of the 'brave new world' is convincing: man can be estimated as having the same value as a machine. In principle he can be rendered wholly functional— and in the end still be happy! The feeling of happiness becomes

[1]German title for the parable of the Prodigal Son, Luke 15: 11–32.

a technological product. To the person who protests against this civilisation and who seeks to reassert the former values of humanity, the leader of the world-government in Huxley's novel can say: But today our people are happy! They are happier than ever before. Do you want to restore their sufferings? Such arguments seem to be irrefutable. Is it not in fact enough when people can experience a maximum of happiness? What more should man strive for on behalf of man and society? Here, however, one factor does seem to have been omitted, and possibly this factor is the decisive one.

'When we reject morality, something elementally biological takes its place: that which holds the promise of pleasure is good; what promises to be displeasing is bad.' This is how Paul Schütz sums up the kind of modern humanism for which the criterion of humanity is the individual's claim to happiness (op. cit., p. 30). This is where he connects the 'omitted factor' with the 'absent God' in an age of the 'eclipse of God' and of the 'death of God'.

'Is it possible that the "absent" God and the "omitted factor" have something to do with one another? "Absent" and "omitted". Where then? It can only be in our consciousness, and not by any means in our experience. Thus it is a "false consciousness", the living of a lie, and it arises from the constant suppression of reality' (p. 30).

When the claim to happiness (or the right to 'self-realisation') is made the criterion of humanity, then what we have called the positive openness of human existence disappears. And when this happens, it is unlikely that any objection will be raised against the 'brave new world'.

But what is meant by the 'dignity of man'? What do we mean by the 'worth of the person'? If one day, we may do with persons as we please, where is the criterion for action to be found? A human society which is unwilling to go the way of the 'brave new world' will thus require a new political and social ideal, *an ideal of the humanity of the future*. In an age in which man has become wholly manipulable, do the traditional human values still hold good?

The notion of humanity must be worked out anew, and this is the fundamental task of every political philosophy. *What is man?*

For the foreseeable future, this will be where faith in God may be seen to have a new and decisive social importance. If it should turn out that we are not in a position to discover a new and acceptable definition of man's humanity; if, practically speaking, it is no longer obvious why man, the person, should deserve the infinite respect which he needs if he is to remain and become the norm for every social and political action; and if it should no longer seem obvious why we should have a boundless hope in man, then faith's worth will be proved.

In this threatening situation the person can remain the norm, or, *if he is even more than what he is*, more than what we can observe and control, and more than what we can manipulate, he can become new. (And it does seem that one day we shall be in a position to manipulate everything.) A machine is no more than what it is. The person, however, must be more than what he is. This 'more' does not mean that by some chance or influence man may possibly become something in the future. This 'more' implies 'fulfilment'. It means that the individual is 'addressed' by another Person, by his Creator—even in the banality and the monotony of his everyday existence. This 'everyman' is 'more than what he is'. This can be grasped when we understand him as existing in the living and creative 'between' between himself and his God. This is the relationship in which 'everyman' stands—a relationship of undreamed-of possibilities.

One does not need to be a Christian in order to recognize, or even to be convinced that this is man's true dignity, namely, that man (indeed *every* man simply as man), is more than his spiritual condition, more than his open (while doubtful) future. One does not have to believe in a personal God to see that neither the maximising of pleasure nor self-realisation can be the true criteria of humanity. The true criterion is what we call the person—inexpressible, impenetrable, fundamentally and uniquely mysterious. And justice is done to persons only through love. The real clue to this, the most illuminating thought which leads to the *true* interpretation of this mystery and which at the same time lays upon us an inescapable demand to live and to act in a human way, is faith in a personal God, in a God who is near to all men and who addresses and loves each one of us.

When the individual, even in the monotony and banality of his life, lives at the same time in the light of God's presence, as long as persons have access for God and room for God, when this is really the subject of our thinking and a matter of experience—then society can always remain and become a human society. As long as man's aim is not simply happiness, then the measure and criterion of humanity will remain established as the relatedness of the person to him who (in Augustine's prayer) is the

> God, from whom to turn
> is to fall,
>
> To whom to turn
> is to rise,
>
> In whom to abide
> is to be safe
>
> God, whom to forsake
> is to die,
>
> To whom to return
> is to awake to newness of life,
>
> In whom to dwell
> is to live for ever.

For Further Reading:

Karl Barth, *Anselm: Fides Quaerens Intellectum*, SCM Press, London, 1960.

Dietrich Bonhoeffer, *Letters and Papers from Prison*, revised and enl. edition, SCM Press, London, 1967.

Emil Brunner, *Truth as Encounter*, SCM Press, London, 1964.

Martin Buber, Various works such as *I and Thou*, Edinburgh, 1937; *Between Man and Man*, Collins Fontana Library, London, 1961; *Eclipse of God*, V. Gollancz, London, 1953.

Rudolf Bultmann, *Jesus Christ and Mythology*, SCM Press, London, 1960.

Gerhard Ebeling, *Gott und Wort*, 1966.

Helmut Gollwitzer, *The Existence of God as confessed by Faith*, SCM Press, London, 1965.

Heinrich Ott, *Wirklichkeit und Glaube*, Vol. II, 1969.

Raimundo Panikkar, *Religionen und die Religion*, Munich, 1965.

John A. T. Robinson, *Honest to God*, SCM Press, London, 1963.

Paul Schütz, *Warum ich noch nicht ein Christ bin*, 3rd ed. 1969.

Dorothee Sölle, *Christ the Representative*, SCM Press, London, 1967. *Atheistisch an Gott glauben*, 1969.

Paul Tillich, *The Courage to be*, Collins Fontana Library, London, 1962. *Systematic Theology*, Vol. I, Jas. Nisbet & Co. London, 1953.

Heinz Zahrnt, *What kind of God?* SCM Press, London, 1971.